The Best of Mr. Food

Weeknight Quickies

"Have I got dinnertime solutions for you! Easy entrées, satisfying sides, and dazzling desserts, all ready to be served up in a jiffy. 'OOH IT'S SO GOOD!!®'"

Beef Fajita Pizza,
page 120

Boiled Shrimp Supper, page 10

Strawberry Shortcake,
page 182

The Best of Mr. Food

Weeknight Quickies

Oxmoor House®

©2006 by Oxmoor House, Inc.
Book Division of Southern Progress Corporation
P.O. Box 2262, Birmingham, Alabama 35201-2262

ISBN-13: 978-0-8487-3116-8
ISBN-10: 0-8487-3116-6
Library of Congress Control Number: 2006926104

Printed in the United States of America
First Printing 2006

Mr. Food® and OOH IT'S SO GOOD!!® are registered marks owned by Ginsburg Enterprises Incorporated.

Ginsburg Enterprises Incorporated
    Chief Executive Officer: Art Ginsburg
    Chief Operating Officer: Steven Ginsburg
    Vice President, Creative Business Development: Howard Rosenthal
    Vice President, Publishing: Caryl Ginsburg Fantel
    Director of Finance and Administration: Nanette Todd

Oxmoor House, Inc.
    Editor in Chief: Nancy Fitzpatrick Wyatt
    Executive Editor: Susan Carlisle Payne
    Copy Chief: Allison Long Lowery

THE BEST OF MR. FOOD® WEEKNIGHT QUICKIES, featuring the recipes of
Mr. Food, Art Ginsburg
    Editor: Kelly Hooper Troiano
    Nutrition Editor: Anne C. Cain, M.S., M.P.H., R.D.
    Senior Copy Editor: L. Amanda Owens
    Editorial Assistant: Brigette Gaucher
    Director, Test Kitchens: Elizabeth Tyler Austin
    Assistant Director, Test Kitchens: Julie Christopher
    Food Stylist: Kelley Self Wilton
    Test Kitchen Professionals: Kristi Carter, Nicole L. Faber, Kathleen Royal Phillips, Elise Weis
    Photography Director: Jim Bathie
    Senior Photo Stylist: Kay E. Clarke
    Photo Stylist: Katherine Eckert
    Director of Production: Laura Lockhart
    Senior Production Manager: Greg Amason
    Production Assistant: Faye Porter Bonner
    Publishing Systems Administrator: Rick Tucker

    Contributors:
    Designer: Rita Yerby
    Indexer: Mary Ann Laurens
    Editorial Assistant: Rachel Quinlivan, R.D.
    Interns: Meg Kozinsky, Ashley Leath, Caroline Markunas,
      Vanessa Rusch Thomas
    Photographer: Lee Harrelson
    Photo Stylist: Katie Stoddard

Cover: *Easy Spaghetti, page 116*

Contents

Welcome!!

"Need a solution to your dinnertime dilemma without resorting to fast food? Check out *Weeknight Quickies* for tasty, wholesome recipes that would have made Mama proud. Turn the pages to discover:

- 2 weeks' worth of menus
- Dishes that can be prepared in 20 minutes or less
- Simple one-dish fares that don't need all the extras
- Recipes for the health conscious
- Easy solutions to round out your meals

From start to finish, you'll never spend more than 45 minutes getting these weeknight favorites on the table—fast! Here's how:

- Each recipe contains easy-to-find ingredients and numbered step-by-step directions
- A game plan for each menu guides you effortlessly through meal preparation
- Prep and cook times make meal planning a breeze
- Recipe tips make cooking a cinch.

And with over 175 recipes to choose from, you'll never have to ask yourself what's for dinner again!"

Mr. Food

Menus in Minutes

"With two weeks' worth of menus, I take the guesswork out of what's for dinner! Check out my game plans for minimizing your time in the kitchen."

dinner menu

- BBQ Meat Loaf
- Garlic Mashed Potatoes
- Salad
- Decadent Mud Pie

Menu

Shrimp Boil

serves 4

Boiled Shrimp Supper
French Bread
Watermelon

Boiled Shrimp Supper

(pictured on page 3)

4 servings

prep: 5 minutes   cook: 30 minutes

3   quarts water
4   (3-ounce) packages boil-in-bag
        shrimp and crab boil
1   teaspoon salt
1½ pounds new potatoes
1   (16-ounce) package frozen pearl or
        boiling onions
8   frozen half-ears corn on the cob
2   lemons, cut in half

1½ pounds unpeeled, large fresh shrimp
Lemon wedges
Cocktail sauce

1 Combine first 3 ingredients in a stockpot or large Dutch oven; bring to a boil. Add potatoes, frozen onions, frozen corn, and lemon halves; return to a boil, and cook 15 minutes or until potatoes are tender.

2 Add shrimp; cover and cook 5 minutes or until shrimp turn pink. Drain mixture; remove and discard seasoning bags and lemon halves. Serve immediately with lemon wedges and cocktail sauce.

Game Plan

1. Put water on to boil with seasoning mixture and salt.

2. Meanwhile, spread butcher paper over table to prepare for the feast.

3. Add vegetables, lemon, and shrimp per recipe directions.

4. Drain mixture, and dump shrimp and vegetables on top of paper on table.

5. Peel shrimp at the table; serve with lemon, cocktail sauce, and French bread.

6. Slice the watermelon—and let the good times roll!

Menu

Soup's On—Mexican Style
serves 4

Spicy Chicken Posole
Tortilla Chips
Chocolate Ice Cream

Spicy Chicken Posole

4 servings

prep: 8 minutes   cook: 18 minutes

1   slice bacon

1   (7-ounce) can chipotle chilies in
        adobo sauce (see note)
2   (4-ounce) skinned and boned
        chicken breasts, chopped

1   small onion, chopped
1   small red bell pepper, chopped
2   cups chicken broth
1   (15.5-ounce) can hominy, drained
½   cup (2 ounces) shredded Monterey
        Jack cheese

Game Plan

1. Cook bacon, and reserve drippings for posole.

2. Chop chicken, onion, bell pepper, and chipotle chili for posole.

3. Cook chicken.

4. Combine posole ingredients, and simmer.

5. Serve posole with tortilla chips, and follow with ice cream.

1 Cook bacon in a Dutch oven until crisp; remove bacon, reserving drippings in pan. Reserve bacon for another use.

2 Remove 1 chipotle chili and 3 tablespoons adobo sauce from can; reserve remaining chilies and sauce for another use. Mince chili, and set aside. Combine chicken and 3 tablespoons adobo sauce.

3 Heat bacon drippings in pan over medium-high heat. Add chicken, and sauté until chicken is browned. Remove chicken; set aside, and keep warm.

4 Add onion and bell pepper to pan; sauté 3 to 4 minutes or until tender. Return chicken to pan; add broth, hominy, and reserved minced chipotle chili. Bring to a boil; reduce heat, and simmer, uncovered, 5 minutes. Top each serving evenly with shredded cheese.

Note: Look for chipotle chilies in the ethnic section of larger supermarkets.

Menu

Dinner at Mama's
serves 8

Beef in Roasted Pepper Gravy
Steamed Green Beans
Caramel-Apple Crumble

Beef in Roasted Pepper Gravy

8 servings

prep: 5 minutes   cook: 20 minutes

1 (12-ounce) package medium egg noodles, uncooked

1 (2¼- to 2½-pound) package refrigerated fully cooked beef pot roast with gravy

1 (14½-ounce) can diced tomatoes with onion and garlic, undrained

1 cup frozen small white onions

1 (7-ounce) jar roasted red bell peppers, drained and chopped

½ teaspoon black pepper

½ cup chopped fresh parsley or 2 tablespoons dried parsley

1 Cook noodles according to package directions.

2 Meanwhile, remove pot roast from package, reserving gravy; add gravy to a 4-quart Dutch oven. Add tomatoes, onions, roasted bell peppers, and black pepper to gravy. Bring gravy mixture to a boil; cover, reduce heat, and simmer 10 minutes.

3 Cut pot roast into 2" pieces. Add to gravy mixture; cover and cook 5 more minutes.

4 Drain noodles; toss with parsley. Serve beef mixture over noodles.

Caramel-Apple Crumble

8 servings

prep: 6 minutes   cook: 12 minutes

2   (20-ounce) cans sliced apples,
        drained
½   teaspoon ground cinnamon
⅓   cup caramel topping

4   cups caramel-praline crunch
        ice cream
4   shortbread cookies, crumbled

1 Place sliced apples in an 8" square microwave-safe baking dish. Sprinkle with cinnamon; drizzle with caramel topping. Cover with plastic wrap, and vent; microwave at HIGH 12 minutes, rotating dish every 4 minutes if your microwave doesn't have a turntable. Cool.

2 Spoon ½ cup ice cream into each of 8 dessert dishes; top each serving with ½ cup apple mixture. Sprinkle crumbled cookies evenly over apple mixture.

Note: This recipe was tested in an 1100-watt microwave.

Game Plan

1. Boil water for noodles.

2. Chop bell peppers and parsley for beef dish.

3. Steam beans in microwave, and cook beef dish while noodles cook.

4. Cook apples in microwave as you sit down to dinner.

5. After dinner, spoon apple mixture over ice cream and serve dessert.

Menu

Dinner for Two
serves 2

Veal Piccata
Squash Sauté
Bakery Rolls

Veal Piccata

2 servings

prep: 5 minutes   cook: 5 minutes

½   pound veal cutlets
Olive oil-flavored nonstick cooking spray
¼   teaspoon salt
¼   teaspoon pepper
¼   cup Italian-seasoned breadcrumbs

2   tablespoons chicken broth
1   tablespoon dry white wine or
        1 tablespoon chicken broth
1   tablespoon lemon juice
1   tablespoon butter
2   tablespoons chopped fresh parsley
        or 2 teaspoons dried parsley

Warm cooked angel hair pasta

1 Place veal between 2 sheets of heavy-duty plastic wrap; flatten to ¼" thickness, using a meat mallet or rolling pin. Coat veal with nonstick cooking spray; sprinkle with salt and pepper. Dredge veal in breadcrumbs.

2 Heat a large nonstick skillet over medium-high heat; add veal. Cook 1 to 2 minutes on each side or until done. Set aside, and keep warm.

3 Reduce heat; add broth, wine, and lemon juice to skillet. Cook 30 seconds, stirring to loosen browned bits. Remove from heat; add butter and parsley, stirring until butter melts.

4 Place pasta evenly on each plate; top evenly with veal and sauce. Serve immediately.

Squash Sauté

2 servings

prep: 2 minutes   cook: 6 minutes

1   teaspoon butter
1   zucchini, diagonally sliced
1   small yellow squash, diagonally
        sliced
1   teaspoon Greek seasoning

1 Melt butter in a large nonstick skillet over medium-high heat. Add zucchini and squash; sauté 2 minutes. Add Greek seasoning; sauté 3 more minutes or until tender.

Game Plan

1. Boil water, and cook pasta.

2. Meanwhile, slice and cook zucchini and squash; keep warm.

3. Prepare veal recipe, and heat rolls.

Menu
Taco Night
serves 6

Turkey Tacos
Hot Pepper Rice

Turkey Tacos

6 servings

prep: 5 minutes   cook: 12 minutes

6   taco shells

1   tablespoon vegetable oil
1¼   pounds ground turkey
¾   cup fresh or frozen chopped onion
½   cup chopped red or green bell
         pepper
1   jalapeño pepper, seeded and
         chopped

1   (1-ounce) envelope dry onion soup
         mix
1   (1¼-ounce) package taco seasoning
         mix
¾   cup water
1   cup chunky salsa

Toppings: shredded Cheddar cheese,
         sour cream, shredded lettuce

1 Heat taco shells according to package directions.

2 Meanwhile, heat oil in a large nonstick skillet over medium-high heat. Add turkey and next 3 ingredients, stirring constantly, until turkey crumbles and is no longer pink.

3 Add soup mix, taco seasoning mix, and water. Cover and cook 5 minutes; uncover and simmer 2 minutes. Stir in salsa, and cook until thoroughly heated.

4 Fill each taco shell evenly with turkey mixture, and top with desired toppings. Serve immediately.

Hot Pepper Rice

6 servings

prep: 6 minutes   cook: 15 minutes

3	cups cooked long-grain rice
1	(8-ounce) container sour cream
1	(4.5-ounce) can chopped green chilies, drained
1	fresh jalapeño pepper, seeded and diced
1	cup (4 ounces) shredded Monterey Jack cheese, divided
1	cup (4 ounces) shredded Cheddar cheese, divided

1 Preheat the oven to 350°. Combine first 4 ingredients. Spoon half of mixture into a lightly greased 1½-quart baking dish.

2 Sprinkle ½ cup each of Monterey Jack cheese and Cheddar cheese over rice mixture in dish. Repeat layers, using remaining rice mixture and cheeses. Bake, uncovered, at 350° for 15 minutes or until mixture is thoroughly heated.

Game Plan

1. Cook rice per package instructions, using boil-in-bag rice, or use leftover rice.

2. Chop jalapeño peppers (for both recipes) and bell pepper; shred lettuce.

3. Mix together ingredients for Hot Pepper Rice, and bake as directed.

4. While rice bakes, cook turkey and vegetables in skillet. Stir in remaining ingredients per recipe directions.

5. Serve tacos with favorite toppings and rice.

Menu
Down-home Favorites
serves 4

Salmon Patties
Parmesan Green Beans

Salmon Patties

4 servings

prep: 12 minutes   cook: 7 minutes

1   (14.75-ounce) can pink salmon
½   cup egg substitute
½   cup crushed saltine crackers (about
        14 crackers)
⅓   cup thinly sliced scallions
1   tablespoon lemon juice
¼   teaspoon salt
¼   teaspoon pepper

Nonstick cooking spray

1 Drain salmon; discard skin and bones. Mix together salmon, egg substitute, and next 5 ingredients in a bowl. Divide mixture into 4 equal portions, shaping each into a ¾"-thick patty.

2 Heat a large nonstick skillet coated with nonstick cooking spray over medium-high heat. Add patties, and cook 3 minutes on each side or until light golden. If desired, serve with cocktail or tartar sauce.

Parmesan Green Beans

4 to 6 servings

prep: 10 minutes   cook: 8 minutes

1½ pounds fresh green beans, trimmed

¼ cup grated Parmesan cheese
¼ cup olive oil
3 tablespoons chopped fresh basil or
      1 tablespoon dried basil
3 tablespoons cider vinegar
1 teaspoon sugar
½ teaspoon salt
¼ teaspoon pepper

1 Cook green beans in boiling salted water to cover 3 to 5 minutes or until crisp-tender.

2 Plunge green beans into ice water to stop the cooking process; drain and set aside.

3 Process Parmesan cheese and remaining 6 ingredients in a food processor until smooth, stopping to scrape down sides.

4 Toss together green beans and dressing. Cover and chill until ready to serve.

Game Plan

1. Prepare vegetables and herbs for both recipes.

2. Cook green beans per recipe directions.

3. Stir together dressing, and toss with green beans. Chill until ready to serve.

4. Prepare salmon patties.

5. Cook salmon patties; serve with cocktail or tartar sauce, if desired.

Menu

South-of-the-Border Brunch
serves 6

Green Chili Brunch Pie
Fresh Fruit
Bakery Sweet Rolls
Mexican Coffee

Green Chili Brunch Pie

6 servings

prep: 5 minutes   cook: 37 minutes

¼	cup all-purpose flour
½	teaspoon baking powder
2	tablespoons butter, melted
5	large eggs
1	(12-ounce) container small-curd cottage cheese
1	(4.5-ounce) can chopped green chilies, undrained
2	cups (8 ounces) shredded Monterey Jack cheese

1 Preheat the oven to 400°. Combine first 4 ingredients in a large mixing bowl; beat at medium speed of an electric beater until well blended.

2 Stir in cottage cheese, chilies, and Monterey Jack cheese; pour into a well-greased 9" pie plate.

3 Bake at 400° for 10 minutes. Reduce oven temperature to 350°; bake 25 to 27 more minutes or until set.

Mexican Coffee

6 cups

prep: 12 minutes   cook: 5 minutes

½   cup ground dark roast coffee
1   tablespoon ground cinnamon
¼   teaspoon ground nutmeg
5   cups water

1   cup milk
⅓   cup chocolate flavor syrup
¼   cup packed dark brown sugar
1   teaspoon vanilla extract
Frozen whipped topping, thawed
Additional ground cinnamon

1 Place coffee in filter basket of a coffeemaker; add 1 tablespoon ground cinnamon and the nutmeg. Add water to coffeemaker; brew coffee according to manufacturer's instructions.

2 Combine milk, chocolate flavor syrup, and sugar in a large saucepan; cook over low heat, stirring constantly, until sugar dissolves. Stir in brewed coffee and vanilla. Pour immediately into mugs, and top each serving with a dollop of whipped topping. Sprinkle with additional ground cinnamon.

Game Plan

1. Prepare pie according to recipe directions.

2. While pie bakes, arrange fresh fruit and sweet rolls on platters.

3. Brew coffee, and prepare Mexican Coffee. Top each serving with whipped topping and a sprinkling of ground cinnamon. Olé! Brunch is served!

Menu

Supper Soirée for Two
serves 2

Tenderloin Steaks with Garlic Sauce
Mashed Sweet Potatoes with Goat Cheese
Steamed Broccoli
Raspberry Sorbet

Tenderloin Steaks with Garlic Sauce

2 servings

prep: 5 minutes   cook: 9 minutes

¼   cup beef broth
2   tablespoons dry red wine
1   tablespoon balsamic vinegar
⅛   teaspoon salt
1   large clove garlic, minced

¼   teaspoon salt
¼   teaspoon coarsely ground pepper
2   (4-ounce) beef tenderloin steaks
        (¾" to 1" thick)

1 Combine first 5 ingredients in a small bowl; set aside.

2 Press ¼ teaspoon salt and the pepper evenly onto steaks. Heat a heavy skillet over high heat. Place steaks in pan; cook 3 minutes on each side or to desired degree of doneness. Transfer steaks to a plate; keep warm.

3 Reduce heat to medium; add broth mixture to skillet. Cook 2 minutes or until sauce is slightly reduced, scraping pan to loosen browned bits. Serve sauce over steaks.

Mashed Sweet Potatoes with Goat Cheese

2 servings

prep: 8 minutes   cook: 15 minutes

½   pound sweet potatoes, peeled and
     cubed

¼   cup (1 ounce) goat cheese
⅛   teaspoon salt
⅛   teaspoon pepper

1 Cook potatoes in a large saucepan in boiling water to cover 10 to 15 minutes or until tender; drain.

2 Return potatoes to pan. Add cheese, salt, and pepper; mash well with a potato masher.

Game Plan

1. Peel and cube sweet potatoes; cook in boiling water, and drain.

2. Trim broccoli, and steam.

3. Cook steaks.

4. Mash sweet potatoes with remaining ingredients.

5. Prepare Garlic Sauce.

6. Serve dinner followed by sorbet for dessert.

Menu

Company's Coming
serves 4

Sage-Crusted Turkey Tenderloin
Wild Rice
Sweet 'n' Sassy Brussels Sprouts
Whole Wheat Rolls
Easy Pecan Tarts (see page 191)

Sage-Crusted Turkey Tenderloin

4 servings

prep: 5 minutes   cook: 25 minutes

3   tablespoons finely chopped fresh
      sage or 1 tablespoon dried sage
3   tablespoons shredded three-cheese
      blend
¼   cup coarsely crushed cornflakes
      cereal
1   (1-pound) package turkey
      tenderloins
1   tablespoon butter, melted
½   teaspoon salt

1 Preheat the oven to 425°. Combine first 3 ingredients in a shallow dish. Brush turkey with melted butter; sprinkle with salt. Dredge turkey in sage mixture, coating well.

2 Place turkey on a lightly greased baking sheet. Bake at 425° for 25 minutes or until meat thermometer registers 170°.

Sweet 'n' Sassy Brussels Sprouts

4 servings

prep: 5 minutes   cook: 7 minutes

16   small Brussels sprouts

⅓   cup orange marmalade

1 Trim ends of sprouts. Place in a 1½-quart microwave-safe dish; add water to cover.

2 Microwave at HIGH 7 minutes or just until tender; drain. Add marmalade, and toss well to coat.

Note: This recipe was tested in an 1100-watt microwave.

Game Plan

1. Stir together tart filling, and spoon into shells.

2. Cook tarts per recipe directions, and cool completely.

3. Chop sage, if using fresh; crush cornflakes cereal.

4. Dredge turkey, and bake.

5. Meanwhile, trim ends of Brussels sprouts.

6. Prepare long-grain and wild rice mix according to package directions.

7. Heat rolls.

8. Microwave Brussels sprouts, and toss with marmalade.

9. Serve dinner, and then top tarts with whipped cream and a pecan half for a special touch.

Menu

Summer Supper
serves 4

Cajun Catfish
Apple-Bacon Coleslaw
Cornbread or Hush Puppies

Cajun Catfish

4 servings

prep: 5 minutes   cook: 10 minutes

4   teaspoons Cajun seasoning
4   (4-ounce) farm-raised catfish fillets
Nonstick cooking spray

4   teaspoons lemon juice

1 Preheat the grill to medium-high heat (350° to 400°). Meanwhile, sprinkle Cajun seasoning on both sides of fillets; lightly coat fish with nonstick cooking spray. Arrange fish in a wire grilling basket coated with cooking spray. Place basket on grill rack; cover and grill 5 minutes.

2 Turn grill basket over; drizzle lemon juice over fish. Cover and grill 5 more minutes or until fish flakes easily with a fork.

Apple-Bacon Coleslaw

4 cups

prep: 10 minutes   chill: 30 minutes

3   tablespoons olive oil
2   tablespoons mayonnaise
1   tablespoon Dijon mustard
1   tablespoon lemon juice
½   teaspoon hot sauce
¼   teaspoon salt

1   (16-ounce) package shredded
      coleslaw mix
1   large Gala apple, peeled and finely
      diced
Freshly ground pepper to taste

4   precooked slices bacon, crumbled

1 Whisk together first 6 ingredients in a large bowl.

2 Add coleslaw mix, apple, and ground pepper, tossing well to coat.

3 Cover and chill 30 minutes. Sprinkle with bacon just before serving.

Game Plan

1. Preheat the grill. Prepare coleslaw, and chill 30 minutes.

2. Prepare choice of bread.

3. Season fish, and grill.

4. Sprinkle bacon over coleslaw just before serving.

Menu

Casual Night
serves 4

Three-Pepper Pork Cutlets
Rice Pilaf
Steamed Asparagus
Cinnamon Ice Cream

Three-Pepper Pork Cutlets

4 servings

prep: 10 minutes   cook: 8 minutes

1   (1-pound) pork tenderloin

1   teaspoon paprika
1   teaspoon dried thyme
½   teaspoon dried oregano
½   teaspoon dried rosemary, crushed
¼   teaspoon salt
¼   teaspoon ground white pepper
¼   teaspoon black pepper
⅛   teaspoon ground red pepper
1   teaspoon olive oil
2   cloves garlic, crushed

1 Preheat the broiler. Cut pork crosswise into 12 slices. Place each pork slice between 2 sheets of heavy-duty plastic wrap, and flatten to ¼" thickness, using a meat mallet or rolling pin.

2 Combine paprika and remaining 9 ingredients; rub over both sides of pork slices. Place pork on a lightly greased rack in a broiler pan. Broil 5½" from heat 3 to 4 minutes on each side or until done.

Cinnamon Ice Cream

4 servings

prep: 7 minutes

1   quart vanilla ice cream, slightly
        softened
1   teaspoon ground cinnamon
Hot fudge topping

1 Stir together ice cream and cinnamon in a large bowl. Refreeze, if desired. Scoop into serving dishes, and drizzle with fudge topping.

Game Plan

1. Soften ice cream, and stir in cinnamon; freeze until serving time.

2. Cook rice pilaf according to package directions, and steam asparagus; keep warm.

3. While side dishes cook, prepare pork.

4. Serve dinner; afterward, scoop ice cream into serving dishes, and top with fudge sauce.

Menu
Weeknight Delight
serves 2

Ham Fried Rice
Steamed Sugar Snap Peas
Mandarin Orange Sections
Almond Cookies

Ham Fried Rice

2 servings

prep: 3 minutes   cook: 12 minutes

2   teaspoons dark sesame oil
½   cup frozen green peas
2   scallions, sliced
1¼   cups cooked long-grain rice, chilled
½   cup diced cooked ham

1   large egg, lightly beaten
2   tablespoons soy sauce
1   tablespoon water

1 Heat oil in a large nonstick skillet over medium-high heat. Add peas and scallions; sauté 3 minutes or until tender. Add rice and ham; cook until thoroughly heated. Push rice mixture to sides of pan, forming a well in center.

2 Add egg to well, and cook until set, stirring egg occasionally. Stir rice mixture into egg mixture. Stir in soy sauce and water.

Game Plan

1. Cook rice using 1 small bag of boil-in-bag rice, or use leftover rice. Chill rice at least 5 to 10 minutes.

2. Slice scallions, dice ham, and trim sugar snap peas.

3. Prepare fried rice.

4. Steam sugar snap peas.

5. Serve dinner; then drain oranges, and spoon into serving dishes. Serve with almond cookies.

Menu

Stir-Fry Night

serves 4

Sweet Pepper-Chicken Stir-Fry
Grissini Breadsticks
Fortune Cookies

Sweet Pepper-Chicken Stir-Fry

4 servings

prep: 8 minutes   cook: 11 minutes

1   to 2 tablespoons light sesame oil or
    vegetable oil
1   pound chicken breast strips

2   tablespoons water
1   (16-ounce) package frozen broccoli,
    carrots, and cauliflower
1   red onion, cut into 8 wedges
2   red bell peppers, seeded and cut
    into thin strips
1   (11.75-ounce) bottle stir-fry sauce
Warm cooked rice

1 Pour oil around top of a preheated wok, coating sides, or in a large non-stick skillet. Heat at medium-high (375°) for 2 minutes. Add chicken, and stir-fry 2 minutes or until light golden.

2 Add water, frozen vegetables, onion, and bell pepper strips, stirring gently. Cover and cook 6 minutes or until vegetables are crisp-tender, stirring once. Add stir-fry sauce; stir-fry 1 minute or until thoroughly heated. Serve over rice.

Game Plan

1. Cook enough rice for 4 servings.

2. Meanwhile, cut up onion and bell peppers. Stir-fry chicken and vegetables.

3. Serve stir-fry over rice and with grissini breadsticks. (They look like chopsticks!)

4. Serve fortune cookies for a fun dessert.

Menu

Cajun Family Favorite
serves 6

Sausage Jambalaya
French Bread
Praline Cream-Pecan Pie (see page 186)

Sausage Jambalaya

6 servings

prep: 10 minutes   cook: 15 minutes

2   large packages boil-in-bag rice, uncooked

1   pound smoked sausage, cut into ¼" diagonal slices
1⅓   cups chopped cooked ham
2   celery ribs, chopped
2   cloves garlic, minced
1   medium onion, chopped

1   (14-ounce) can beef broth
½   teaspoon black pepper
½   teaspoon ground red pepper (optional)

1 Prepare rice according to package directions. Drain and keep warm.

2 Meanwhile, combine sausage and next 4 ingredients in a Dutch oven. Cook over medium-high heat, stirring constantly, until sausage is browned.

3 Add broth, black pepper, and, if desired, red pepper to Dutch oven; bring mixture to a boil. Reduce heat, and simmer, uncovered, 5 minutes, stirring occasionally. Stir in cooked rice.

Game Plan

1. Bake pie according to package directions.
2. Prepare whipped cream mixture for pie, and chill until ready to serve.
3. Prepare rice. Meanwhile, start preparing and cooking other ingredients for jambalaya.
4. Stir cooked rice into jambalaya, and serve with French bread.
5. To serve pie, drizzle servings with praline liqueur; top with whipped cream mixture.

20-Minute Miracles

"Food on the table in 20 minutes from start to finish? You betcha! Turn the page to see how.**"**

Fast Clam Chowder

4 servings

prep: 3 minutes   cook: 15 minutes

2   tablespoons butter
1   medium onion, chopped

1⅓ cups milk
1   (10¾-ounce) can cream of potato
      soup, undiluted
1   (6½-ounce) can minced clams,
      undrained

1 Melt butter in a large saucepan over medium heat. Add onion; sauté, stirring constantly, until onion is tender.

2 Add milk and remaining ingredients, stirring until blended. Bring to a boil over medium heat; reduce heat, and simmer, uncovered, 10 minutes.

Chowder Chatter
There are 2 main types of chowder—Manhattan style that's tomato based and New England style, like ours, that's milk based.

Cream of Peanut Soup

6 servings

prep: 5 minutes   cook: 15 minutes

¼   cup butter
1   small onion, finely chopped
⅔   cup finely chopped celery
2   tablespoons all-purpose flour

2   cups chicken broth
1   cup milk
1   cup half-and-half
1   cup creamy peanut butter
Salt and pepper to taste
Paprika

1 Melt butter in a large saucepan over medium-high heat. Add onion and celery; cook, stirring constantly, until tender. Reduce heat to low; add flour, stirring until blended. Cook 1 minute, stirring constantly.

2 Gradually add chicken broth and milk; cook over medium heat, stirring constantly, until mixture is thickened and bubbly. Stir in half-and-half and peanut butter; cook 5 minutes, stirring constantly. Add salt and pepper to taste; sprinkle with paprika.

❝Sautéed vegetables, chicken broth, and seasonings turn a normally sweet ingredient into a potful of savory goodness.❞

Bean 'n' Veggie Soft Tacos

(pictured on facing page)

6 servings

prep: 15 minutes   cook: 5 minutes

½   teaspoon ground cumin
½   cup Italian dressing

1   zucchini, shredded
1   yellow squash, shredded
½   red bell pepper, chopped
1   small onion, chopped

1   (15-ounce) can black beans, rinsed
      and drained
¼   cup water
1   teaspoon Adobo seasoning
      (see note)

6   (6") flour tortillas, warmed
1   cup (4 ounces) shredded Monterey
      Jack cheese with peppers

1 Whisk together cumin and Italian dressing in a large bowl.

2 Add zucchini and next 3 ingredients; toss gently. Set aside.

3 Combine black beans and next 2 ingredients in a saucepan. Bring to a boil; reduce heat, and simmer 3 minutes or until thoroughly heated.

4 Spoon zucchini mixture evenly down center of each tortilla. Top evenly with bean mixture and cheese. Roll up tortillas; secure each with a wooden toothpick. Garnish with coarsely chopped fresh cilantro, if desired.

Note: Look for Adobo seasoning in the ethnic section of larger supermarkets. Or create a similar blend with ½ teaspoon chili powder and ¼ teaspoon each of salt, garlic powder, and dried crushed red pepper.

On a Roll
Warming tortillas in the microwave or oven according to package directions makes them pliable and easy to roll up.

Quick Beef with
Broccoli, page 54

Chicken-Avocado Dagwoods,
page 150

Browned Butter-Chicken Fettuccine

(pictured on facing page)

4 servings

prep: 10 minutes   cook: 10 minutes

12 ounces dried fettuccine, uncooked

½   cup butter
4   skinned and boned chicken breasts,
       cut into strips
1   clove garlic, crushed
1   (2¼-ounce) package slivered
       almonds, toasted (see tip)

½   cup chopped fresh parsley
2   tablespoons dry white wine or
       2 tablespoons chicken broth
1   teaspoon lemon juice
½   teaspoon salt
¼   cup grated Parmesan cheese

1 Cook pasta according to package
  directions; drain and keep warm.

2 Meanwhile, melt butter in a large
  skillet over medium-high heat,
swirling skillet until butter is browned.
Add chicken, garlic, and almonds; cook
4 minutes or until chicken is done.

3 Stir in parsley and next 3 ingredients;
  toss with warm cooked pasta. Sprinkle
with cheese, and serve immediately.

Nut Pointers
Toasting brings out the full flavor of nuts. To toast these
almonds, cook them in a dry skillet over medium heat
until you begin to smell their aroma, stirring often. Watch
'em closely! The smaller the pieces, the quicker they cook.

Turkey Breast Marsala

8 servings

prep: 3 minutes   cook: 12 minutes

¼   cup butter, melted
8   (½"-thick) slices cooked turkey
       breast (about 1½ pounds)
⅛   teaspoon pepper

8   slices prosciutto (about ¼ pound)
8   (1-ounce) slices Monterey Jack
       cheese
½   cup Marsala (see note)

1 Melt butter in a large skillet over medium-high heat. Add turkey, and brown 2 minutes on each side. Sprinkle with pepper.

2 Place 1 slice of prosciutto and 1 slice of cheese on top of each slice of turkey. Pour Marsala over cheese.

3 Cover, reduce heat to medium-low, and cook until cheese melts.

Note: You can substitute ½ cup white grape juice or ½ cup dry white wine plus 1 teaspoon brandy for Marsala.

❝Have the deli slice your turkey, prosciutto, and cheese for you. It'll save on prep time, and you'll have perfectly even slices!❞

Garlic Scampi

4 servings

prep: 9 minutes   cook: 15 minutes

| 8 | ounces dried angel hair pasta, uncooked |

½   cup butter
4   large cloves garlic, minced
1   pound peeled, medium-sized fresh shrimp (1⅓ pounds unpeeled)
⅓   cup dry white wine or ⅓ cup chicken broth
¼   teaspoon freshly ground pepper

¾   cup grated Parmesan or Romano cheese
¼   cup chopped fresh parsley or 1 tablespoon dried parsley

1 Cook pasta according to package directions; drain and place on a large serving platter.

2 Meanwhile, melt butter in a large skillet over medium-high heat. Add garlic and shrimp; cook, stirring constantly, 3 to 5 minutes or until shrimp turn pink. Add wine and pepper. Bring to a boil; cook, stirring constantly, 30 seconds.

3 Remove from heat; stir in cheese and parsley. Pour shrimp mixture over pasta; toss gently. Serve immediately.

“This buttery-sauced shrimp is over the top! Try it over French bread, rice, or egg noodles, too. Yum-my!”

Oven-Baked Salmon Steaks

4 servings

prep: 3 minutes   cook: 12 minutes

4   (6-ounce) salmon steaks
¼   cup butter, melted
1   teaspoon lemon-pepper seasoning
1   teaspoon garlic salt
1   teaspoon paprika

Lemon wedges

1 Preheat the oven to 500°. Place salmon steaks in a 7" x 11" baking dish. Combine butter, lemon-pepper seasoning, and garlic salt in a small bowl; stir well. Pour over steaks in dish. Sprinkle with paprika.

2 Bake, uncovered, at 500° for 10 to 12 minutes or until fish flakes easily with a fork. Serve with lemon wedges.

M-m-m! Fresh salmon never had it so good—and neither have you, I bet! It's a cinch to slather this easy-to-make herbed butter over the salmon steaks, and pop 'em in the oven.

Tex-Mex Pepper Steak

4 servings

prep: 5 minutes   cook: 15 minutes

2   (3.5-ounce) bags boil-in-bag rice

¾   pound flank steak
2   teaspoons chili powder
1   teaspoon ground cumin
¼   teaspoon salt

2   tablespoons olive oil, divided
1   (16-ounce) package frozen bell
        pepper stir-fry
1   (14½-ounce) can Mexican-style
        stewed tomatoes, undrained

Wrap It Up
Wrap this juicy meat mixture
in a flour tortilla for additional
Tex-Mex flavor.

1 Prepare rice according to package
directions to make 4 cups cooked
rice.

2 While rice cooks, slice steak in half
lengthwise; slice each half diagonally
across grain into ¼"-thick slices. Combine
chili powder, cumin, and salt in a resealable plastic freezer bag; add meat. Seal
bag, and shake until meat is well coated.

3 Heat 1 tablespoon oil in a large nonstick skillet over medium-high heat.
Add meat; stir-fry 4 minutes or until
browned.

4 Remove meat from skillet, and set
aside; add remaining 1 tablespoon oil
to skillet, and heat over medium heat.
Add bell pepper stir-fry; stir-fry 2 minutes
or just until tender. Add tomatoes; bring
to a boil. Cook 2 minutes, stirring occasionally. Return meat to skillet; cook
until thoroughly heated. Remove skillet
from heat.

5 To serve, place 1 cup rice on each
of 4 plates; top evenly with meat
mixture.

Tuscan Pork Chops

4 servings

prep: 8 minutes   cook: 12 minutes

¼   cup all-purpose flour
1   teaspoon salt
¾   teaspoon seasoned pepper
4   (1"-thick) boneless pork chops

1   tablespoon olive oil

3   to 4 cloves garlic, minced
⅓   cup balsamic vinegar
⅓   cup chicken broth
3   plum tomatoes, seeded and diced
2   tablespoons capers

1 Combine first 3 ingredients in a shallow dish; dredge pork chops in flour mixture.

2 Heat oil in a large nonstick skillet over medium-high heat. Add chops, and cook 1 to 2 minutes on each side or until golden. Remove chops from skillet.

3 Add garlic to skillet, and sauté 1 minute. Add vinegar and broth, stirring to loosen particles from bottom of skillet; stir in tomatoes and capers.

4 Return chops to skillet; bring sauce to a boil. Cover, reduce heat, and simmer 4 to 5 minutes or until chops are done. Serve chops with tomato mixture.

❝For an even quicker prep time, use a handy jar of already minced garlic. One-half teaspoon equals 1 clove of garlic.❞

Parmesan Pork Tenderloin

4 servings

prep: 5 minutes   cook: 10 minutes

1 (1-pound) pork tenderloin, cut into
    1"-thick slices (see tip)

3 tablespoons Italian-seasoned
    breadcrumbs
1 tablespoon grated Parmesan cheese
1 teaspoon salt
1/8 teaspoon pepper

2 teaspoons vegetable oil
1 small onion, chopped
1 clove garlic, minced

1 Place pork between 2 sheets of heavy-duty plastic wrap; flatten to 1/2" thickness, using a meat mallet or rolling pin.

2 Combine breadcrumbs and next 3 ingredients in a shallow dish; stir well. Dredge pork in breadcrumb mixture, coating well.

3 Heat oil in a large skillet over medium heat. Add pork, onion, and garlic; cook about 10 minutes or until pork is done, turning pork once.

❝Flattening the pork medallions to the same thickness enables them to cook evenly—and more quickly!❞

Spicy Couscous

4 servings

prep: 3 minutes   cook: 8 minutes

1   cup chicken broth
¼   cup sliced scallions
1   (4.5-ounce) can chopped green
    chilies, undrained

⅔   cup couscous, uncooked (see note)

1 Combine first 3 ingredients in a medium saucepan; bring to a boil.

2 Remove saucepan from heat, and stir in couscous. Cover and let stand 5 minutes. Fluff with a fork before serving.

Note: Couscous is a tiny pasta that is made from semolina wheat. It's a great alternative to rice and is gaining popularity because it cooks so quickly—in 5 minutes!

Taste the Difference
Chicken broth adds flavor to rice, grits, and—as done here—couscous. When any grain recipe calls for water, you can generally substitute an equal amount of broth.

Italian Green Beans and Potatoes

8 servings

prep: 5 minutes   cook: 12 minutes

1   tablespoon butter
½   cup chopped onion
½   cup chopped green bell pepper

1   (16-ounce) can whole new potatoes,
       drained and sliced
1   (14½-ounce) can stewed tomatoes,
       undrained
1   (16-ounce) can cut Italian green
       beans, drained
¼   cup grated Parmesan cheese

1 Melt butter in a large skillet over medium-high heat; add onion and bell pepper, and sauté, stirring constantly, until tender.

2 Add potatoes, and sauté 2 more minutes. Add stewed tomatoes and beans, and cook until thoroughly heated. Sprinkle with cheese. Serve immediately.

Canned Goodness

Canned veggies are a cinch to prepare and take on new flair in this colorful side dish. They retain comparable nutrients to fresh vegetables because they go straight from the garden to the cannery—no extensive traveling for these nutritious gems. If you're watching your sodium intake, look for low-sodium versions because regular canned veggies contain quite a bit of salt.

Provençale Tomatoes

4 servings

prep: 4 minutes   cook: 10 minutes

2   medium tomatoes, halved crosswise
2   teaspoons Dijon mustard
¼   teaspoon pepper
¼   cup Italian-seasoned breadcrumbs
2   teaspoons olive oil

1 Preheat the oven to 450°. Place tomato halves cut sides up in a greased baking dish. Spread top of each tomato half with ½ teaspoon mustard; sprinkle evenly with pepper and bread-crumbs. Drizzle with oil.

2 Bake at 450° for 10 minutes or until tops are golden.

"Fresh tomatoes are available year-round—but no doubt about it, the most prized are vine-ripened, right-off-the-plant tomatoes! They are at their peak from June through September. You'll enjoy the taste of Provence with each bite of these babies—no matter what the season!"

Banana Split Pudding

4 servings

prep: 10 minutes

3 bananas, thinly sliced (see tip)
1 cup fresh strawberries, sliced
1 cup whipping cream

¼ cup fudge sauce
2 tablespoons crunchy peanut butter

1 Reserve 4 banana slices and 8 strawberry slices for garnish. Beat remaining banana slices in a mixing bowl at medium speed of an electric beater until smooth. Add whipping cream; beat until soft peaks form (mixture will not beat to stiff peaks).

2 Combine fudge sauce and peanut butter; fold into whipped cream mixture. Gently fold in remaining strawberry slices. Spoon evenly into 4 (8-ounce) parfait glasses. Top with reserved fruit slices. Serve immediately.

No More Brown Bananas!

For this recipe and others, prevent banana slices from turning brown by tossing them with a mixture of 1 tablespoon of lemon juice per 1 cup of water.

Wafflewiches

4 servings

prep: 5 minutes

1   cup chocolate frozen yogurt, slightly
     softened

4   frozen waffles, toasted

2   tablespoons chocolate sauce

2   tablespoons chopped nuts

1 Spread ½ cup softened frozen yogurt over each of 2 toasted waffles. Top with remaining 2 toasted waffles.

2 Cut each wafflewich into 4 wedges, and drizzle 2 tablespoons chocolate sauce evenly over wedges. Sprinkle evenly with nuts.

66You may want to pull out the forks and knives to eat these ooey-gooey frozen yogurt sandwiches!99

One-Dish Wonders

66Let one-dish meals be your answer to the dinnertime dilemma. Forget all the extras, 'cause all ya need is in one dish. Now that's sooo easy!99

Quick Beef with Broccoli

(pictured on page 38)

2 servings

prep: 18 minutes   cook: 11 minutes

½	pound flank steak or boneless top round, trimmed
10	sun-dried tomato slices or halves (packed without oil)
¾	cup boiling water
2	teaspoons cornstarch
¼	cup soy sauce
1½	teaspoons sugar

Nonstick cooking spray
2	cups fresh broccoli florets
3	scallions, sliced
1	clove garlic, minced

Warm cooked rice

1 Slice steak diagonally across the grain into very thin slices.

2 Combine tomato slices and boiling water; let stand 5 minutes. Drain and slice tomatoes into thin strips, reserving liquid.

3 Combine cornstarch, soy sauce, sugar, and reserved tomato liquid, stirring until smooth. Set aside.

4 Heat a large nonstick skillet coated with nonstick cooking spray over medium-high heat. Add steak, and cook, stirring constantly, 3 minutes. Remove from skillet, and set aside. Add broccoli; cover and cook 3 minutes. Add tomato strips, scallions, and garlic. Cook, stirring constantly, 3 minutes. Add cornstarch mixture and steak; cook, stirring constantly, 1 minute. Serve over rice.

Fresh vs. Frozen

A thawed 10-ounce package of frozen broccoli florets can also be used in place of fresh broccoli. Add it with the tomatoes, scallions, and garlic; cook, uncovered, 3 minutes, stirring constantly.

Reuben Casserole

8 servings

prep: 10 minutes   cook: 35 minutes

1	(32-ounce) jar sauerkraut, drained
1	medium onion, finely chopped
1¼	cups sour cream
¼	teaspoon garlic powder
4	(2.5-ounce) packages thinly sliced corned beef, cut into thin strips
2½	cups (10 ounces) shredded Swiss cheese
8	slices rye bread
2	tablespoons butter, melted

1 Preheat the oven to 350°. Press sauerkraut between paper towels to remove excess moisture.

2 Combine sauerkraut, onion, sour cream, and garlic powder; stir well. Spoon mixture into a lightly greased 9" x 13" baking dish. Sprinkle corned beef evenly over sauerkraut mixture; top with cheese.

3 Remove crusts from bread; cut each slice in half diagonally. Arrange bread triangles over cheese, completely covering top of casserole; brush with melted butter. Bake at 350° for 35 minutes or until bread is lightly browned.

I've turned a favorite sandwich into a family-pleasin' casserole. It contains all the ingredients and flavors of a traditional Reuben. So what are you waiting for? Dig in!

Speedy Shepherd's Pie

6 servings

prep: 5 minutes cook: 14 minutes

½ (22-ounce) package frozen mashed
      potatoes (about 3 cups)
1⅓ cups milk

1 pound ground round
1 cup fresh or frozen chopped onion
1 cup frozen green peas and carrots
½ teaspoon pepper
1 (12-ounce) jar beef gravy

½ cup (2 ounces) shredded Cheddar
      cheese

1 Combine potatoes and milk in a microwave-safe bowl. Microwave at HIGH, uncovered, 8 minutes, stirring once; set aside.

2 Meanwhile, cook beef and onion in a 10" ovenproof skillet over medium heat, stirring until the beef crumbles and is no longer pink. Add peas and carrots, pepper, and gravy. Cook over medium heat 3 minutes or until thoroughly heated, stirring often; remove mixture from heat.

3 Preheat the broiler. Spoon potatoes evenly over meat mixture, leaving a 1" border around edge of skillet. Broil 5½" from heat 3 minutes or until bubbly. Sprinkle with cheese; let stand 5 minutes.

Note: Mashed potatoes were tested in an 1100-watt microwave oven.

"My version of this traditional English dish is served up pronto, thanks to handy convenience products, such as jarred gravy and frozen veggies."

Enchilada Casserole

8 servings

prep: 15 minutes   cook: 25 minutes

2   pounds ground chuck
1   medium onion, chopped

2   (8-ounce) cans tomato sauce
1   (11-ounce) can Mexicorn, drained
1   (10-ounce) can enchilada sauce
1   teaspoon chili powder
¼   teaspoon ground cumin
½   teaspoon pepper
¼   teaspoon salt

10   (5") corn tortillas, divided
2   cups (8 ounces) shredded Cheddar
     cheese, divided

1 Cook beef and onion in a large skillet over medium-high heat, stirring until the beef crumbles and is no longer pink; drain.

2 Preheat the oven to 375°. Stir tomato sauce and next 6 ingredients into meat mixture; bring to a boil. Reduce heat to medium, and cook, uncovered, 5 minutes, stirring occasionally.

3 Place half of tortillas in bottom of a greased 9" x 13" baking dish. Spoon half of beef mixture over tortillas; sprinkle with 1 cup cheese. Repeat layers with remaining tortillas and the beef mixture.

4 Bake at 375° for 10 minutes. Sprinkle with remaining cheese; bake 5 more minutes or until cheese melts. Serve with sour cream, if desired.

Heat It Up

Add a little heat to this dish by substituting equal amounts of Monterey Jack cheese with peppers for the Cheddar. Green chili peppers add nice color as well as a bit more spice!

Hamburger-Mushroom Pizza

6 servings

prep: 8 minutes   cook: 15 minutes

6   ounces lean ground beef

1   (16-ounce) loaf unsliced Italian bread
½   cup pizza sauce
8   (⅛"-thick) onion slices, separated
        into rings
1   cup sliced fresh mushrooms

1   teaspoon dried Italian seasoning
½   teaspoon garlic powder
¼   teaspoon dried crushed red pepper
1½   cups (6 ounces) shredded pizza
        cheese blend

1 Cook beef in a large nonstick skillet over medium-high heat, stirring until it crumbles and is no longer pink. Drain and pat dry with paper towels.

2 Preheat the oven to 425°. Cut bread in half horizontally. Place both halves cut sides up on a baking sheet. Spread evenly with pizza sauce; top with onion slices, mushrooms, and beef.

3 Stir together Italian seasoning, garlic powder, and red pepper; sprinkle over pizzas. Top evenly with shredded cheese.

4 Bake at 425° for 10 minutes or until cheese melts. Serve immediately.

Crusty Wisdom

Instead of traditional pizza crust, we used a loaf of Italian bread as the base to turn out this pizza in a jiffy. Pita bread rounds also make good crusts, as do other traditional—and fast—crusts, such as Italian bread shells and canned refrigerated pizza crusts.

Skillet Lasagna

4 servings

prep: 5 minutes   cook: 40 minutes

½ pound ground round
½ teaspoon salt
2 tablespoons balsamic vinegar
2 teaspoons dried Italian seasoning, divided
1 cup part-skim ricotta cheese
4 uncooked lasagna noodles, broken into large pieces

1 (14.5-ounce) can diced tomatoes with onions, undrained
1 (12-ounce) jar roasted red bell peppers, drained and chopped
½ cup water
5 teaspoons commercial pesto

¾ cup (3 ounces) mozzarella-Parmesan cheese blend

1 Combine beef and salt. Cook beef in a large nonstick skillet over medium-high heat, stirring until it crumbles and is no longer pink. Stir in vinegar and 1 teaspoon Italian seasoning. Dollop ricotta cheese by rounded tablespoons over beef. Top with broken noodles, making 1 flat layer (noodles will overlap a little bit).

2 Pour tomatoes and bell peppers over noodles, making sure that noodles are completely covered. Add water, and sprinkle with remaining 1 teaspoon Italian seasoning. Dollop pesto by ½ teaspoons over top. Bring mixture to a boil. Cover, reduce heat, and simmer 30 minutes or until noodles are fully cooked.

3 Uncover and sprinkle with cheese blend. Cover and let stand 10 minutes or until cheese melts. Cut into wedges, and serve with a slotted spatula.

No need to dirty up a bunch of dishes for this lasagna, 'cause it all cooks right in the skillet—even the lasagna noodles! Now, that's what I call convenient.

One-Pot Pasta

4 servings

prep: 10 minutes   cook: 28 minutes

1	pound lean ground beef
1	teaspoon vegetable oil
1	small onion, diced
1	(8-ounce) package sliced fresh mushrooms
2	cloves garlic, minced
2	(26-ounce) jars tomato-basil pasta sauce
1	cup water
1	tablespoon dried Italian seasoning
½	teaspoon salt
¼	teaspoon pepper
1	(20-ounce) package refrigerated four-cheese ravioli
1	cup (4 ounces) shredded mozzarella cheese

1 Cook beef in a Dutch oven over medium-high heat, stirring until it crumbles and is no longer pink; drain. Wipe Dutch oven clean.

2 Heat oil in Dutch oven over medium-high heat; add onion and mushrooms, and sauté 8 minutes or until tender. Add garlic, and sauté 1 minute. Stir in beef, pasta sauce, water, and next 3 ingredients.

3 Bring sauce to a boil; add ravioli. Reduce heat to medium-low; cover and simmer, stirring occasionally, 8 to 10 minutes or until pasta is done. Stir in cheese. Serve immediately.

Convenience Matters

With the help of your favorite spaghetti sauce and refrigerated ravioli, you can have dinner on the table lickety-split! Round out your meal with a tossed salad and garlic bread—all conveniently available (already prepared) at your local supermarket.

Hamburger Stroganoff

4 servings

prep: 5 minutes   cook: 25 minutes

1   pound ground chuck
4   slices bacon, chopped
1   small onion, chopped

1   (10¾-ounce) can cream of
        mushroom soup, undiluted
½   teaspoon salt
¼   teaspoon paprika
1   (8-ounce) carton sour cream
Warm cooked egg noodles

1 Cook first 3 ingredients in a large skillet over medium-high heat, stirring until the beef crumbles and is no longer pink; drain.

2 Stir soup, salt, and paprika into beef mixture. Cook, uncovered, over medium heat 15 minutes, stirring occasionally. Stir in sour cream; cook until thoroughly heated. (Do not boil.) Serve beef mixture over noodles.

❝My stroganoff will be a winner with the kiddies! They'll love the hamburger—and you'll love the convenience and ease!❞

Southwest Pork in Black Bean Sauce

6 servings

prep: 15 minutes   cook: 15 minutes

1   tablespoon ground cumin
1   teaspoon Adobo seasoning
        (see note)
1¼ pounds boneless pork loin chops,
        cut into ½" cubes

2   (10-ounce) cans mild diced tomatoes
        and green chilies
1   (15-ounce) can black beans, rinsed
        and drained
1   (8-ounce) can whole kernel corn,
        drained

1   tablespoon vegetable oil
1   cup uncooked instant rice

1   cup (4 ounces) grated Cheddar
        cheese
2   tablespoons chopped fresh cilantro

1 Combine cumin and Adobo seasoning in a large resealable plastic bag.
Remove 2 teaspoons cumin mixture, and
reserve. Add pork to plastic bag. Seal
and shake to coat; set aside.

2 Stir together reserved 2 teaspoons
cumin mixture, the diced tomatoes
and green chilies, black beans, and corn
in a large bowl.

3 Heat vegetable oil in a large skillet over
medium-high heat. Add pork; sauté 6
to 8 minutes or until pork is browned. Stir
in tomato mixture; bring mixture to a boil,
and stir in rice. Cover and remove from
heat. Let stand 5 minutes.

4 Sprinkle evenly with Cheddar cheese
and chopped fresh cilantro. Serve
with flour tortillas and lime wedges, if
desired.

Note: Look for Adobo seasoning in the
ethnic section of large supermarkets.

Savvy Substitutes

Boneless rib-end pork chops
work well here, too. And you
can reduce the heat of this dish
by substituting a can of regular
diced tomatoes for one of the
cans of diced tomatoes and
green chilies.

Fiesta Cabbage

6 servings

prep: 15 minutes   cook: 25 minutes

1   pound kielbasa, cut into ¼"-thick
      slices

1   medium-sized red onion, diced
1   medium-sized green bell pepper,
      diced
1   medium-sized cabbage (about 2½
      pounds), chopped into bite-sized
      pieces

1   (14½-ounce) can diced tomatoes,
      undrained
1   teaspoon salt
½   teaspoon black pepper

1 Heat a large nonstick skillet over medium-high heat. Add kielbasa, and sauté until browned. Remove sausage with a slotted spoon, and drain on paper towels, reserving drippings in skillet. Set aside.

2 Sauté onion and bell pepper in hot drippings in skillet over medium-high heat 3 minutes. Stir in cabbage; cover and cook 15 minutes or until vegetables are tender, stirring occasionally.

3 Stir in cooked sausage, tomatoes, salt, and black pepper. Cook until thoroughly heated.

Crazy for Cabbage

This affordable veggie is easy to prepare. It's also full of flavor, as well as high in fiber, minerals, and vitamins—including vitamin C. Choose a cabbage that's heavy for its size, with crisp, tightly packed leaves. It can be stored in a resealable plastic bag in the fridge for up to 2 weeks.

Baked Ziti

8 servings

prep: 9 minutes   cook: 23 minutes

1   pound mild Italian sausage, casings removed
½   pound ground chuck
1   small onion, chopped
12   ounces ziti, cooked according to package directions
4   cups marinara sauce

1   pound sliced mozzarella cheese, divided
¼   cup grated Parmesan cheese

1 Preheat the oven to 375°. Cook first 3 ingredients in a Dutch oven over medium-high heat, stirring until the meat crumbles and is no longer pink; drain. Stir in pasta and marinara sauce.

2 Spoon half of meat mixture into a greased 9" x 13" baking dish; top with half of mozzarella and remaining meat mixture. Bake, uncovered, at 375° for 10 minutes or until heated. Top with remaining mozzarella and the Parmesan; bake 5 more minutes or until cheeses melt.

Pasta Pointer

Add a tablespoon of vegetable oil to the cooking water to keep the pasta from sticking together and to prevent the water from foaming up and over the sides of the pan.

Hot 'n' Spicy Chicken Dinner

4 to 6 servings

prep: 8 minutes cook: 24 minutes

2   cups uncooked instant rice
2   (10-ounce) cans diced tomatoes and
        green chilies, undrained
1   (10¾-ounce) can Cheddar cheese
        soup, undiluted
1   small onion, chopped
1   teaspoon dried basil
½   teaspoon salt
⅛   teaspoon pepper
2   pounds chicken legs and thighs,
        skinned

1 Combine all ingredients except chicken; pour mixture into a greased microwave-safe 8" x 11" baking dish. Arrange chicken over rice mixture, and cover loosely with wax paper.

2 Microwave, covered, at HIGH 15 minutes. Turn chicken pieces over. Microwave, uncovered, at HIGH 9 minutes or until chicken is done.

Note: This recipe was tested in an 1100-watt microwave oven.

If time is not an issue, this casserole can easily be baked in a conventional oven, uncovered, at 350° for 45 minutes. Either way you cook it up, it's mighty tasty!

Chicken Cacciatore

4 servings

prep: 10 minutes   cook: 20 minutes

2	tablespoons vegetable oil
4	skinned and boned chicken breasts, cut into 1" pieces
½	cup chopped onion
2	cups spaghetti sauce
1½	cups water
1	green bell pepper, seeded and cut into strips
½	teaspoon dried oregano
½	teaspoon dried basil
1½	cups uncooked instant rice

1 Heat oil in a large skillet over medium-high heat. Add chicken and onion; cook until chicken is lightly browned, stirring often.

2 Add spaghetti sauce and next 4 ingredients; stir well. Bring mixture to a boil; stir in rice. Cover, remove from heat, and let stand 5 minutes or until liquid is absorbed and rice is tender.

Quick Italian

Cacciatore is Italian for "hunter." This version of the popular stewlike dish is prepared "hunter-style," using onion and herbs. The prepared spaghetti sauce makes it come together easy—and quick!

Chicken Fricassee

6 servings

prep: 13 minutes   cook: 20 minutes

¼ cup all-purpose flour
6 skinned and boned chicken breasts
¼ cup butter, divided

2 cups sliced fresh mushrooms
3 carrots, sliced

1 (1-ounce) envelope herb-with-lemon
    soup mix
1 cup half-and-half
½ cup water or white wine
2 teaspoons chicken bouillon granules
    or 2 chicken bouillon cubes

1 Place flour in a shallow dish; dredge chicken in flour. Melt 2 tablespoons butter in a large skillet over medium heat; brown chicken in butter. Remove from skillet, and set aside.

2 Melt remaining 2 tablespoons butter in skillet. Add mushrooms and carrots; cook over medium heat, stirring constantly, 4 minutes or until tender.

3 Combine soup mix and remaining 3 ingredients in a medium bowl; pour over mushroom mixture. Bring to a boil, stirring constantly. Add chicken; reduce heat, and simmer 10 minutes or until chicken is done.

Parlez-Vous Français?

Fricassee is the French term for a thick, chunky, stewlike dinner of browned chicken or meat that's simmered with vegetables. Our version delivers that great flavor and convenience in a one-dish meal—fast!

Chicken 'n' Rice Skillet

4 servings

prep: 5 minutes   cook: 22 minutes

1⅓ cups milk
1   (10¾-ounce) can cream of
        mushroom soup, undiluted
1   (6-ounce) package uncooked quick-
        cooking long-grain and wild rice
        mix (including seasoning packet)

1   tablespoon butter, melted
4   skinned and boned chicken breasts

1 Combine milk, soup, rice mix, and seasoning packet; set aside.

2 Melt butter in a large skillet over medium-high heat. Add chicken, and cook 5 minutes on each side. Pour rice mixture over chicken; bring to a boil. Cover, reduce heat, and simmer 12 minutes or until chicken is done and liquid is absorbed.

66*For a quick side salad, purchase a bag of gourmet salad mix, toss in a few cherry tomato halves for color, drizzle with your favorite Italian dressing, and—voilà—dinner is served!*99

Southwestern BBQ Chicken Pizza

4 to 6 servings

prep: 5 minutes   cook: 10 minutes

1   (16-ounce) package prebaked Italian
       cheese-flavored pizza bread shell
½   cup barbecue sauce, divided

2   (9-ounce) packages precooked
       Southwest-flavored chicken breast
       strips, chopped
1½ cups (6 ounces) shredded Mexican
       four-cheese blend
2   tablespoons chopped fresh cilantro

1 Preheat the oven to 450°. Place bread shell on a large baking sheet; spread ¼ cup barbecue sauce over crust.

2 Combine remaining ¼ cup barbecue sauce and the chicken in a bowl, coating well. Spoon chicken mixture over shell; top with cheese and cilantro.

3 Bake at 450° for 10 minutes or until cheese melts.

Pizza Pronto!
Using prepared chicken and pizza crust gets this recipe on the table in only 15 minutes.

Chicken à la King in a Hurry

2 servings

prep: 4 minutes   cook: 10 minutes

1   cup chopped cooked chicken
¼   cup milk
¼   cup frozen green peas, thawed
½   teaspoon salt
¼   teaspoon pepper
1   (10¾-ounce) can cream of chicken
       soup, undiluted
1   (4-ounce) can sliced mushrooms,
       drained
1   (2-ounce) jar diced pimiento, drained

4   slices whole wheat bread, toasted
Paprika

1 Combine first 8 ingredients in a large saucepan; cook over low heat 10 minutes, stirring often.

2 For each serving, cut each slice of toast in half, if desired. Spoon chicken mixture evenly over toast. Sprinkle with paprika.

Toast Points
Feel free to use any kind of bread that you have on hand for the toast. And for a touch of fancy schmancy, diagonally cut your toast into triangles.

Santa Fe Chicken 'n' Dressing

4 to 6 servings

prep: 15 minutes   cook: 30 minutes

3   cups cornbread stuffing mix
2   cups chopped cooked chicken
1   (4.5-ounce) can chopped green
       chilies, drained
½   (7-ounce) jar roasted red bell
       peppers, drained and chopped
2   teaspoons ground coriander
1   (10¾-ounce) can cream of
       mushroom soup, undiluted
1   (8¾-ounce) can cream-style corn
1   (8-ounce) container sour cream
2   teaspoons ground cumin

1   cup (4 ounces) shredded Monterey
       Jack cheese

1 Preheat the oven to 350°. Stir together first 5 ingredients in a large bowl; stir in soup and next 3 ingredients. Spread in a lightly greased 2-quart shallow baking dish.

2 Bake, covered, at 350° for 25 minutes or until thoroughly heated. Uncover and sprinkle evenly with cheese; bake 5 more minutes or until cheese melts. If desired, serve with tortilla chips and pico de gallo or chunky salsa.

"This isn't your ordinary chicken and dressing! Green chilies and roasted bell peppers, along with coriander and cumin, lend a Southwestern flair to this flavor-packed dish. It's another winner!"

Bistro Grilled Chicken Pizza

6 servings

prep: 15 minutes   cook: 10 minutes

Olive oil-flavored nonstick cooking spray
1   (13.8-ounce) can refrigerated pizza
        crust

¾   cup pizza sauce
4   plum tomatoes, sliced
2   cups chopped cooked chicken
1   (4-ounce) package tomato-and-basil
        feta cheese
1   cup (4 ounces) shredded mozzarella
        cheese
2   tablespoons chopped fresh basil

1 Preheat the grill to medium heat (300° to 350°). Line a baking sheet with heavy-duty aluminum foil; coat with nonstick cooking spray. Unroll dough; starting at center, press out dough with hands to form a 9" x 13" rectangle; coat dough evenly with cooking spray.

2 Invert dough onto grill rack; peel off foil. Grill, covered, 2 to 3 minutes or until bottom of dough is golden. Remove dough from grill, and coat with cooking spray; turn dough over, and grill, covered, 1 to 2 minutes or until bottom is set. Carefully remove crust from grill to aluminum foil-lined baking sheet.

3 Microwave pizza sauce in a small glass bowl at HIGH 30 seconds or until warm, stirring once. Spread sauce evenly over crust; top with tomatoes and chicken. Sprinkle evenly with cheeses and basil. Return pizza to grill rack (pizza should slide easily). Grill, covered, 3 to 5 more minutes or until crust is done and cheese melts.

Flipping Over Pizza

We found that using 2 expandable spatulas made it easier to flip the dough on the grill than using just a regular spatula. If you don't have them, a large baking sheet with no sides or long-handled grilling tongs and a spatula will work, too.

Ramen Egg Foo Yong

6 servings

prep: 19 minutes   cook: 17 minutes

2   (3-ounce) packages chicken-flavored
      ramen noodle soup mix

6   large eggs
2   cups finely chopped cooked chicken
½   cup sliced scallions
½   teaspoon salt
½   teaspoon pepper
2   cloves garlic, crushed
1   (8-ounce) can sliced water chestnuts,
      drained and finely chopped

Nonstick cooking spray

2   tablespoons vegetable oil
2   tablespoons all-purpose flour
2   tablespoons soy sauce

1 Prepare soup mix according to package directions; drain noodles, reserving broth. Set aside.

2 Beat eggs in a large bowl until blended. Stir in noodles, chicken, and next 5 ingredients.

3 Heat a large nonstick skillet coated with nonstick cooking spray over medium-high heat. For each patty, carefully pour about ½ cup noodle mixture into skillet. Cook until eggs are set and patties are lightly browned. Remove to a hot ovenproof platter; keep warm. Repeat procedure with remaining noodle mixture.

4 Whisk together oil, flour, and soy sauce in skillet; gradually whisk in reserved broth. Cook, stirring constantly, 2 to 3 minutes or until mixture is thickened. Serve over patties.

"*Shhh! Soup mix is my secret to jump-starting this classic Asian-American dish.*"

Shrimp Creole

3 to 4 servings

prep: 8 minutes   cook: 10 minutes

2   tablespoons butter
½   cup chopped green bell pepper
¼   cup chopped celery
4   scallions, thinly sliced
1   clove garlic, minced

1   (14½-ounce) can Cajun-style stewed
        tomatoes, undrained
1   (6-ounce) can tomato paste
½   cup chicken broth
2   teaspoons dried parsley flakes
½   teaspoon salt
¼   teaspoon ground red pepper

1   pound peeled, medium-sized fresh
        shrimp (1⅓ pounds unpeeled)
Warm cooked rice

1 Melt butter in a large skillet over medium-high heat; add bell pepper and next 3 ingredients. Cook, stirring constantly, 4 minutes.

2 Add tomatoes and next 5 ingredients; cook 2 minutes over medium heat.

3 Add shrimp, and cook 4 minutes or until shrimp turn pink. Serve over rice.

In a Flash!
Make this dish even quicker by using a 16-ounce package of frozen peeled cooked shrimp in place of fresh shrimp. And instead of chopping your vegetables, use a cup of frozen seasoning blend with bell peppers, celery, and onions.

Tortilla Pie

6 servings

prep: 11 minutes   cook: 25 minutes

1   (15-ounce) can black beans, rinsed
       and drained
1   teaspoon chili powder
½   teaspoon ground cumin

8   (8") flour tortillas
1   cup chunky salsa
2   (4-ounce) cartons guacamole
1   (8-ounce) package shredded
       Mexican four-cheese blend

1 Preheat the oven to 350°. Combine first 3 ingredients in a small bowl, stirring well.

2 Place 1 tortilla in a lightly greased 9" round cakepan; spread with half of bean mixture, and top with another tortilla. Spread with half of salsa, and top with another tortilla. Spread with half of guacamole, and top with another tortilla. Sprinkle with half of cheese, and top with another tortilla. Repeat layers with remaining ingredients, except cheese. (Pan will be full.)

3 Cover and bake at 350° for 20 minutes; uncover and sprinkle with remaining cheese. Bake, uncovered, 3 to 5 more minutes. Cut into wedges to serve. If desired, serve with sour cream and additional salsa and guacamole.

❝This meatless entrée is layered with colorful ingredients that tempt your eye just as much as your appetite! Feel free to add a cup of shredded cooked chicken over the first layer of beans for those die-hard meat lovers in your family!❞

Zesty Veggie Pizza

3 to 4 servings

prep: 8 minutes   cook: 15 minutes

1   (16-ounce) package prebaked Italian
      pizza bread shell
1   tablespoon olive oil
½   cup packaged shredded carrots
1   zucchini, sliced
1   clove garlic, minced

1   (11.5-ounce) jar black bean dip
½   cup chunky salsa
1   cup (4 ounces) shredded Monterey
      Jack cheese with peppers

1 Preheat the oven to 350°. Bake bread shell on a baking sheet at 350° for 5 minutes. Meanwhile, heat oil in a skillet over medium heat. Add carrots, zucchini, and garlic; cook, stirring constantly, 3 to 5 minutes or until vegetables are crisp-tender.

2 Spread bean dip over bread shell; top with salsa and vegetables. Sprinkle with cheese. Bake at 350° for 10 minutes or until cheese melts.

66Vegetables star in this yummy pizza. Serving it is a great way to get your 'five (or more) a day!'99

Three-Cheese Spaghetti

2 servings

prep: 5 minutes   cook: 15 minutes

1   tablespoon butter
1   tablespoon all-purpose flour
1   cup milk
½   cup (2 ounces) shredded Swiss
        cheese
½   cup (2 ounces) shredded Gouda
        cheese
¼   teaspoon salt
1   (4½-ounce) jar sliced mushrooms,
        drained

1   (7.3-ounce) package spaghetti,
        uncooked
2   tablespoons butter, melted
½   cup grated Parmesan cheese
1   tablespoon dried parsley flakes

1 Melt 1 tablespoon butter in a heavy saucepan over low heat; add flour, stirring until smooth. Cook, stirring constantly, 1 minute. Gradually add milk; cook over medium heat, stirring constantly, until mixture is thickened and bubbly. Remove from heat; add Swiss cheese, Gouda cheese, salt, and mushrooms, stirring until cheeses melt.

2 Meanwhile, cook spaghetti according to package directions; drain. Combine spaghetti, 2 tablespoons melted butter, the Parmesan cheese, and parsley flakes; toss well. Combine cheese sauce and spaghetti mixture, stirring well.

Watched Pot Won't Boil?
If you're in a hurry for the water to boil, place a saucepan over high heat and cover with a lid. This causes a quicker buildup of steam and pressure—resulting in a faster boil.

Black Bean-Chili Potatoes

4 servings

prep: 8 minutes   cook: 20 minutes

4   large baking potatoes (about
        3 pounds)

Nonstick cooking spray
1   tablespoon vegetable oil
3   cloves garlic, crushed
1   medium onion, chopped
1   (14½-ounce) can chili-style chunky
        tomatoes, undrained
1   (15-ounce) can black beans, rinsed
        and drained
1   teaspoon chili powder
½   teaspoon ground cumin
4   scallions, sliced

1   cup (4 ounces) shredded Cheddar
        cheese
Sour cream (optional)

1 Scrub potatoes; prick each potato several times with a fork. Arrange potatoes 1" apart on a microwave-safe rack or on paper towels. Microwave at HIGH 20 minutes, turning and rearranging after 10 minutes. Let stand 2 minutes.

2 Meanwhile, coat a large saucepan or skillet with nonstick cooking spray; add oil. Place over medium-high heat until hot. Add garlic and onion; cook, stirring constantly, until tender. Stir in tomatoes and next 3 ingredients; cook over medium heat just until thoroughly heated, stirring occasionally. Remove from heat, and stir in scallions.

3 Cut an X to within ½" of bottom of each baked potato. Squeeze potatoes from opposite ends to open; fluff pulp with a fork. Spoon bean mixture over potatoes, and sprinkle with cheese. Top each potato with sour cream, if desired, and serve immediately.

Note: The potatoes were tested in an 1100-watt microwave oven.

This loaded spud satisfies even the hungriest of guys. And if you have some leftover chili of your own, go ahead and pile it high atop a baked potato.

Light Favorites

"It's easy to watch your waistline while still enjoying these quick and oh-so-satisfying recipes!"

Spinach-Red Pepper Crostini

about 26 crostini

prep: 15 minutes   cook: 10 minutes

1 (8-ounce) French baguette, cut
   diagonally into ¼"-thick slices

1 (10-ounce) package frozen chopped
   spinach, thawed

½ cup shredded Parmesan cheese
¼ cup walnuts, toasted (see tip)
3 tablespoons fat-free mayonnaise
2 tablespoons fat-free milk
¼ teaspoon salt
¼ teaspoon black pepper
1 large clove garlic

1 (7-ounce) jar roasted red bell
   peppers, drained and cut into
   thin strips

1 Preheat the oven to 375°. Bake bread slices on a baking sheet at 375° for 5 minutes; set aside.

2 Drain spinach well, pressing between paper towels.

3 Process spinach, Parmesan cheese, and next 6 ingredients in a food processor until mixture is smooth. Spread spinach mixture evenly over bread slices.

4 Bake at 375° for 5 minutes. Top evenly with red bell pepper strips. Serve immediately.

Per slice: CALORIES 41 (31% from fat); FAT 1.4g (sat 0.4g, mono 0.3g, poly 0.5g); PROTEIN 2g; CARBOHYDRATE 5.4g; FIBER 0.4g; CHOLESTEROL 1mg; IRON 0.5mg; SODIUM 144mg; CALCIUM 36mg

Toasty Walnuts
To toast walnuts, spread on a baking sheet and bake at 350° for 5 to 10 minutes, stirring occasionally. Substitute ¼ cup pecans, if desired.

Minestrone

10 servings

prep: 6 minutes   cook: 20 minutes

2   teaspoons olive oil
2   cloves garlic, minced
3   (14-ounce) cans ⅓-less-sodium
       chicken broth
1   (16-ounce) package frozen
       Italian-style vegetables
1   (16-ounce) can pinto beans, rinsed
       and drained
1   (14½-ounce) can Italian-style diced
       tomatoes, undrained
¾   cup (3 ounces) tubetti or other small
       tubular pasta
1½ teaspoons dried Italian seasoning

3   tablespoons plus 1 teaspoon grated
       Parmesan cheese

1 Heat oil in a large saucepan over medium heat. Add garlic, and cook 1 minute or until light golden. Stir in chicken broth and next 5 ingredients. Bring to a boil; reduce heat, and simmer, uncovered, 15 minutes or until pasta is tender.

2 Ladle into individual serving bowls, and sprinkle each serving with 1 teaspoon Parmesan cheese.

Per 1-cup serving: CALORIES 119 (15% from fat); FAT 2g (sat 0.5g, mono 0.9g, poly 0.3g); PROTEIN 7g; CARBOHYDRATE 19.3g; FIBER 3.9g; CHOLESTEROL 1mg; IRON 2.2mg; SODIUM 507mg; CALCIUM 62mg

66This Italian soup helps pack in your daily quota of vegetables—1 cup offers 2 servings of the fruits and veggies you need a day!99

Chicken Tenders Salad

4 servings

prep: 15 minutes   cook: 20 minutes

¼ cup all-purpose flour
½ teaspoon pepper
1 pound chicken tenders

3 tablespoons fat-free egg substitute
⅓ cup fat-free milk
1 cup Italian-seasoned breadcrumbs
3 tablespoons sesame seeds

Nonstick cooking spray

1 (10-ounce) package romaine lettuce, torn
2 large tomatoes, cut into wedges
¼ cup (1 ounce) shredded reduced-fat Cheddar cheese

1 Preheat the oven to 425°. Combine flour and pepper in a large resealable plastic freezer bag. Add chicken tenders; seal bag, and shake to coat.

2 Combine egg substitute and milk in a shallow dish, stirring well. Combine breadcrumbs and sesame seeds in another shallow dish.

3 Dip each chicken tender in egg mixture, and dredge in breadcrumb mixture. Place in a single layer on a baking sheet coated with nonstick cooking spray. Coat chicken tenders with cooking spray. Bake, uncovered, at 425° for 20 minutes or until done. Cut chicken diagonally into 1" pieces.

4 Place ½ cup lettuce on each of 4 plates. Divide chicken and tomatoes evenly among plates. Top each serving with 1 tablespoon cheese. Serve with reduced-fat salad dressing.

Per serving (undressed): CALORIES 361 (21% from fat); FAT 8.4g (sat 2g, mono 1.7g, poly 2g); PROTEIN 37g; CARBOHYDRATE 34.8g; FIBER 4.7g; CHOLESTEROL 71mg; IRON 4.8mg; SODIUM 537mg; CALCIUM 229mg

❝Make extra chicken tenders for the kids if salad isn't their thing. These tenders are oh-so-good just by themselves! Don't forget the light honey-mustard or ranch dressing for dipping.❞

Canadian BLTs

4 servings

prep: 9 minutes   cook: 8 minutes

8   slices Canadian bacon

⅓   cup reduced-fat sour cream
1   tablespoon fat-free Italian dressing
8   (1-ounce) slices rye bread, toasted

4   leaves romaine lettuce
8   (¼") slices tomato
Freshly ground pepper

1 Cook bacon in a nonstick skillet over medium heat 4 minutes or until lightly browned. Set aside.

2 Combine sour cream and Italian dressing in a small bowl; stir well. Spread evenly on 1 side of each bread slice.

3 Layer bacon, lettuce, and tomatoes evenly on 4 bread slices. Sprinkle with pepper. Top with remaining bread slices.

Per serving: CALORIES 287 (27% from fat); FAT 8.6g (sat 3.2g, mono 3.4g, poly 1g); PROTEIN 17.7g; CARBOHYDRATE 34.3g; FIBER 4.3g; CHOLESTEROL 35mg; IRON 2.4mg; SODIUM 1,181mg; CALCIUM 77mg

❝Leaner Canadian bacon replaces regular bacon in my light version of the classic sandwich.❞

Steak au Poivre

2 servings

prep: 3 minutes   cook: 16 minutes

1	tablespoon cracked black pepper
2	(4-ounce) beef tenderloin steaks (1" thick)

Nonstick cooking spray

¼	cup brandy
½	cup beef broth
¼	teaspoon salt
¼	teaspoon sugar
3	tablespoons reduced-fat sour cream

1 Press cracked black pepper evenly onto both sides of steaks.

2 Heat a large nonstick skillet coated with nonstick cooking spray over medium-high heat. Add steaks, and cook 5 minutes on each side or to desired degree of doneness. Transfer to a serving platter; set aside, and keep warm.

3 Add brandy to skillet; let simmer 30 seconds or until liquid is reduced to a glaze. Add beef broth, salt, and sugar. Simmer, uncovered, 4 to 5 minutes or until liquid is reduced by half.

4 Remove skillet from heat; stir in sour cream. Serve sauce with steak.

Per serving: CALORIES 216 (40% from fat); FAT 9.5g (sat 4.2g, mono 3.4g, poly 0.4g); PROTEIN 20.4g; CARBOHYDRATE 4g; FIBER 0.8g; CHOLESTEROL 62mg; IRON 3.3mg; SODIUM 771mg; CALCIUM 42mg

❝This fancy schmancy French dish features steak that's generously covered in cracked pepper. It's perfect for a romantic dinner.❞

Mini BBQ Meat Loaves

(pictured on page 106)

4 servings

prep: 7 minutes   cook: 25 minutes

1   pound ground round
½   cup plus 2 tablespoons barbecue
        sauce, divided
¼   cup frozen chopped onion, pressed
        dry
⅓   cup quick-cooking oats
1   egg
¼   teaspoon pepper

1 Preheat the oven to 425°. Combine beef, ½ cup barbecue sauce, the onion, and remaining 3 ingredients in a large bowl; stir well.

2 Shape mixture into 4 mini loaves. Place loaves on a lightly greased rack in a broiler pan. Bake at 425° for 20 minutes. Spread remaining 2 tablespoons barbecue sauce evenly over loaves; bake 5 more minutes. Let stand 5 to 10 minutes before slicing.

Per serving: CALORIES 207 (28% from fat); FAT 6.4g (sat 2.1g, mono 2.4g, poly 1.1g); PROTEIN 27.3g; CARBOHYDRATE 10.7g; FIBER 1.3g; CHOLESTEROL 113mg; IRON 2.8mg; SODIUM 401mg; CALCIUM 20mg

❝Serve up these meat loaves with Garlic Mashed Potatoes (page 94) and steamed green beans, and you'll make a meal reminiscent of home—minus the large number of calories and fat!**❞**

Fennel Roasted Pork

4 servings

prep: 9 minutes   cook: 20 minutes

Nonstick cooking spray

1   (¾-pound) pork tenderloin
1   teaspoon fennel seeds, crushed
¼   teaspoon salt
¼   teaspoon pepper

⅔   cup chopped Granny Smith apple
      (about ½ of a small apple)
⅓   cup apple juice
¼   cup sliced leeks or scallions
¼   cup apple juice
2   teaspoons cornstarch

Crushed Seeds

No problem if you don't have a mortar and pestle around. A bowl and the handle of an ice-cream scoop work nicely to crush fennel seeds, as would any rounded kitchen tool you have available.

1 Coat cold grill rack with nonstick cooking spray. Prepare a hot fire or lava rocks on one side of grill, leaving other side empty. Place rack on grill; let grill preheat for 10 to 15 minutes.

2 Meanwhile, trim fat from tenderloin. Combine fennel seeds, salt, and pepper. Rub mixture on all sides of tenderloin. Place tenderloin over empty side of grill; grill, covered, 20 minutes or until a meat thermometer inserted into thickest part of tenderloin registers 155°. Remove from grill, and let stand 10 minutes or until thermometer registers 160°.

3 While meat cooks, combine apple, ⅓ cup apple juice, and the leeks in a saucepan. Bring to a boil; cover, reduce heat, and simmer 5 minutes. Combine ¼ cup apple juice and the cornstarch; stir well. Add cornstarch mixture to leek mixture. Bring to a boil; reduce heat, and simmer, stirring constantly, 1 minute or until thickened.

4 Thinly slice pork. Serve with apple and leek mixture.

Per serving: CALORIES 129 (20% from fat); FAT 2.8g (sat 0.9g, mono 1.2g, poly 0.3g); PROTEIN 16.7g; CARBOHYDRATE 8.7g; FIBER 0.7g; CHOLESTEROL 51mg; IRON 1.4mg; SODIUM 188mg; CALCIUM 17mg

Chicken 'n' Dumplings

6 servings

prep: 10 minutes   cook: 15 minutes

Nonstick cooking spray
3   celery ribs, sliced
2   carrots, sliced
3   (14-ounce) cans low-sodium,
        fat-free chicken broth
½   teaspoon poultry seasoning
½   teaspoon pepper

1⅔ cups reduced-fat biscuit baking mix
⅔   cup fat-free milk

3   cups chopped cooked chicken

1 Heat a large Dutch oven coated with nonstick cooking spray over medium-high heat; sauté celery and carrots 6 minutes or until tender. Stir in broth, poultry seasoning, and pepper; bring to a boil.

2 Meanwhile, stir together baking mix and milk until blended. Turn dough out onto a heavily floured surface; roll or pat dough to a ⅛" thickness. Cut into 2" x 3" strips.

3 Drop strips 1 at a time into boiling broth; stir in chicken. Cover, reduce heat, and simmer 8 minutes, stirring occasionally.

Per serving: CALORIES 276 (21% from fat); FAT 6.5g (sat 1.6g, mono 2.7g, poly 1.7g); PROTEIN 20.7g; CARBOHYDRATE 27.2g; FIBER 1.1g; CHOLESTEROL 51mg; IRON 1.2mg; SODIUM 476mg; CALCIUM 65mg

❝*I'm betting the farm that my lightened version of this down-home classic will become a favorite with your gang. No flavor was sacrificed here—just calories and time!***❞**

Glazed Chicken Thighs

8 servings

prep: 10 minutes   cook: 15 minutes

1   cup pineapple juice
2   tablespoons brown sugar
1   tablespoon light soy sauce
1   teaspoon cornstarch

¾   teaspoon salt
½   teaspoon pepper
2   pounds skinned and boned chicken
     thighs
3   tablespoons all-purpose flour

Nonstick cooking spray
1   tablespoon butter

1 Whisk together first 4 ingredients until smooth; set aside.

2 Sprinkle salt and pepper evenly over chicken. Dust evenly with flour.

3 Coat a large nonstick skillet with non-stick cooking spray. Melt butter over medium-high heat. Add chicken, and cook 5 to 6 minutes on each side. Remove chicken from pan, and keep warm. Add pineapple juice mixture to skillet; cook, whisking constantly, 1 minute or until thickened and bubbly. Pour over chicken.

Per serving: CALORIES 182 (29% from fat); FAT 5.9g (sat 2g, mono 1.8g, poly 1.1g); PROTEIN 22.8g; CARBOHYDRATE 7.9g; FIBER 0.2g; CHOLESTEROL 98mg; IRON 1.4mg; SODIUM 407mg; CALCIUM 18mg

The Thighs Have It

Give chicken breasts a rest, and serve up this sweet-and-tangy dish with chicken thighs. Thighs do have a slightly higher fat content than breasts, but with the skin removed, thighs have less total fat than the same amount of beef tenderloin, sirloin pork chop, or salmon. Plus, they're widely available already skinned and boned. And thighs rule when it comes to flavor!

Cheese-Stuffed Swordfish

4 servings

prep: 15 minutes   cook: 10 minutes

1   (1-pound) swordfish fillet
2   ounces part-skim mozzarella cheese,
      cut into 4 equal slices
Olive oil-flavored nonstick cooking spray

3   tablespoons grated Parmesan
      cheese
2   tablespoons fine, dry breadcrumbs
      (store-bought)
1   tablespoon minced fresh parsley or
      1 teaspoon dried parsley
1   tablespoon drained capers, minced
½   teaspoon ground pepper
1   clove garlic, minced

1 Cut fillet into 4 equal pieces; cut a pocket in each piece, cutting to, but not through, remaining 3 sides. Place cheese slices into pockets; secure openings with wooden toothpicks. Coat fillets with nonstick cooking spray.

2 Combine Parmesan cheese and remaining 5 ingredients in a shallow dish; mix well. Dredge fillets in breadcrumb mixture.

3 Coat cold grill rack with cooking spray; preheat grill to medium-high heat (350° to 400°). Place fillets on rack; grill, covered, 5 minutes on each side or until fish flakes easily with a fork. Serve immediately.

Per serving: CALORIES 210 (38% from fat); FAT 8.9g (sat 3.7g, mono 2.1g, poly 1.2g); PROTEIN 28.1g; CARBOHYDRATE 3.7g; FIBER 0.3g; CHOLESTEROL 58mg; IRON 1.2mg; SODIUM 360mg; CALCIUM 158mg

Make-Ahead Tip
If you're cooking for company, stuff the fish before they arrive and chill in the refrigerator. Right before dinnertime, coat the fish with the crumb mixture and grill for 10 minutes.

Trout with Almonds

4 servings

prep: 6 minutes   cook: 8 minutes

¼   cup all-purpose flour
¼   teaspoon salt
¼   teaspoon pepper
4   (4-ounce) trout fillets

3   tablespoons yogurt-based spread,
       divided (see note)

2   tablespoons chopped fresh parsley
       or 2 teaspoons dried parsley
2   tablespoons lemon juice
¼   cup slivered almonds, toasted
       (see tip on page 41)

1 Combine first 3 ingredients in a large resealable plastic freezer bag. Add fillets; seal bag, and turn gently to coat.

2 Melt 1 tablespoon spread in a large nonstick skillet over medium-high heat. Add fillets to skillet; cook, turning once, 5 to 6 minutes, or until fish flakes easily with a fork. Set fillets aside, and keep warm.

3 Add remaining 2 tablespoons spread, the parsley, and lemon juice to skillet; bring to a simmer. Spoon sauce over fillets; sprinkle with almonds.

Note: Look for yogurt-based spread in the dairy section near the butter.

Per serving: CALORIES 222 (46% from fat); FAT 11.4g (sat 2.2g, mono 4g, poly 3.6g); PROTEIN 21.3g; CARBOHYDRATE 8.2g; FIBER 1.1g; CHOLESTEROL 94mg; IRON 1.1mg; SODIUM 280mg; CALCIUM 41mg

Healthy Fats

You may notice that this recipe is higher in fat than most fish entrées, but the fats here are mostly monounsaturated and polyunsaturated—the good heart-healthy kinds. And compared with traditional trout almondine, which has about 54 grams of fat, no worries!

Crab Cakes

4 servings

prep: 15 minutes   cook: 12 minutes

1 pound fresh lump crabmeat, drained
1½ cups soft breadcrumbs (homemade)
¼ cup chopped scallions
1 tablespoon chopped fresh parsley or
   1 teaspoon dried parsley
2 tablespoons reduced-calorie
   mayonnaise
1½ teaspoons Dijon mustard
1½ tablespoons lemon juice
1½ teaspoons Worcestershire sauce
1 teaspoon ground pepper
¼ teaspoon hot sauce
2 egg whites, lightly beaten

Nonstick cooking spray
2 teaspoons vegetable oil, divided

1 Stir together first 11 ingredients in a medium bowl. Shape mixture into 8 (½"-thick) patties.

2 Coat a large nonstick skillet with non-stick cooking spray; add 1 teaspoon oil, and place over medium heat until hot. Place 4 patties in skillet, and cook 3 minutes on each side or until golden. Repeat procedure with remaining 1 teaspoon oil and 4 patties.

Per serving (2 patties): CALORIES 204 (29% from fat); FAT 6.6g (sat 1g, mono 1.9g, poly 3.1g); PROTEIN 23.8g; CARBOHYDRATE 11g; FIBER 0.8g; CHOLESTEROL 88mg; IRON 1.7mg; SODIUM 578mg; CALCIUM 138mg

66Most of the preparation time here is spent picking through the crabmeat to remove bits of cartilage from the flakes. I guarantee that after one bite of these you'll agree it was worth the effort!99

Shrimp with Roasted Red Pepper Cream

6 servings

prep: 10 minutes   cook: 13 minutes

1   (7-ounce) package vermicelli

1   (12-ounce) jar roasted red bell
       peppers, drained
1   (8-ounce) package ⅓-less-fat cream
       cheese, softened
½   cup low-sodium, fat-free chicken
       broth
3   cloves garlic, chopped
½   teaspoon ground red pepper

2   pounds peeled, large cooked shrimp
¼   cup chopped fresh basil

1 Prepare pasta according to package directions, omitting salt and oil. Set aside, and keep pasta warm.

2 Meanwhile, process bell peppers and next 4 ingredients in a blender or food processor until smooth, scraping down sides. Pour mixture into a large skillet.

3 Cook pepper mixture over medium heat 5 minutes until thoroughly heated, stirring often. Add shrimp, and cook 2 to 3 minutes or until thoroughly heated, stirring occasionally. Remove from heat. Serve over warm cooked pasta. Sprinkle with chopped basil.

Per serving: CALORIES 353 (18% from fat); FAT 6.8g (sat 2.8g, mono 0.4g, poly 1.2g); PROTEIN 40.2g; CARBOHYDRATE 30g; FIBER 1.5g; CHOLESTEROL 243mg; IRON 5mg; SODIUM 530mg; CALCIUM 123mg

Time-saver
Save time by buying the cooked and peeled shrimp at the seafood counter. If you'd rather cook and peel your own, you'll want to start with 4 pounds of raw shrimp in the shell.

Gingered Asparagus

6 servings

prep: 5 minutes   cook: 9 minutes

2   teaspoons vegetable oil
1½ pounds fresh asparagus, trimmed

2   teaspoons minced fresh or jarred
       ginger (see tip)
½   teaspoon sugar
¼   teaspoon salt
¼   teaspoon pepper
1   teaspoon sesame oil

1 Heat vegetable oil in a large nonstick skillet over medium-high heat. Add asparagus, and sauté 7 minutes.

2 Add ginger, and sauté 1 minute. Stir in sugar and remaining ingredients, and cook 1 minute.

Per serving: CALORIES 53 (40% from fat); FAT 2.3g (sat 0.3g, mono 1g, poly 1g); PROTEIN 2.5g; CARBOHYDRATE 5.4g; FIBER 2.5g; CHOLESTEROL 0mg; IRON 0.5mg; SODIUM 97mg; CALCIUM 25mg

Stock It Up

Store up on fresh ginger the next time you're at the supermarket. Buy several large pieces, grate all of it, and keep it in a resealable plastic freezer bag. It can be stored in the freezer for several months and is ready when you need it. Jarred ginger is also available. Look for it in the produce or ethnic foods section of your supermarket. If you use jarred ginger in this recipe, stir it in with the sugar and remaining ingredients, and just cook for 1 minute.

Garlic Mashed Potatoes

(pictured on page 106)

4 servings

prep: 3 minutes   cook: 5 minutes

2⅔ cups frozen mashed potatoes
1⅓ cups fat-free milk
¼ teaspoon salt
¼ teaspoon pepper
¼ teaspoon garlic powder

1 Combine all ingredients in a medium-sized microwave-safe bowl. Cook according to package microwave directions.

Per serving: CALORIES 84 (1% from fat); FAT 0.1g (sat 0.1g, mono 0g, poly 0g); PROTEIN 3.9g; CARBOHYDRATE 15.3g; FIBER 2.3g; CHOLESTEROL 2mg; IRON 0mg; SODIUM 196mg; CALCIUM 103mg

Pump It Up

We pumped up the flavor of frozen mashed potatoes with simple ingredients you probably have on hand. For more flavor boosters, add chopped scallions, shredded low-fat cheese, reduced-fat bacon, or a flavored spreadable cheese.

Hash Brown Casserole

8 servings

prep: 5 minutes   cook: 30 minutes

1   (10¾-ounce) can reduced-fat,
        reduced-sodium cream of
        mushroom soup, undiluted
½   cup (2 ounces) shredded reduced-fat
        sharp Cheddar cheese
½   cup light sour cream
¼   cup chopped scallions
¼   cup fat-free milk
⅛   teaspoon ground red pepper
⅛   teaspoon ground nutmeg (optional)
½   (32-ounce) package frozen hash
        brown potatoes
Butter-flavored nonstick cooking spray

½   cup crushed cornflakes cereal

1 Preheat the oven to 350°. Combine first 6 ingredients in a large bowl, stirring well. Stir in nutmeg, if desired. Stir in hash brown potatoes; pour into a 7" x 11" baking dish coated with nonstick cooking spray.

2 Sprinkle with crushed cornflakes; coat cornflakes with cooking spray. Bake, uncovered, at 350° for 30 minutes or until bubbly. Serve immediately.

Per serving: CALORIES 176 (39% from fat); FAT 7.7g (sat 3.8g, mono 2.2g, poly 0.7g); PROTEIN 5g; CARBOHYDRATE 23.6g; FIBER 1.3g; CHOLESTEROL 12mg; IRON 2.2mg; SODIUM 243mg; CALCIUM 97mg

Helping Hands

Let the kids help you out with this recipe—it'll be a smashing success! Measure out 1⅓ cups of cornflakes cereal in a resealable plastic freezer bag. Seal the bag, and then let the kids crush the flakes with their hands or a rolling pin.

Sweet Potato Casserole

4 servings

prep: 7 minutes   cook: 30 minutes

1   (14.5-ounce) can mashed sweet
     potatoes
2   tablespoons brown sugar
2   tablespoons fat-free milk
2   teaspoons reduced-calorie
     margarine, melted
¼   teaspoon salt
Nonstick cooking spray

¼   cup packed brown sugar
2   tablespoons all-purpose flour
1   tablespoon reduced-calorie
     margarine
2   tablespoons chopped pecans

1 Preheat the oven to 350°. Combine first 5 ingredients in a bowl; stir well. Spoon sweet potato mixture into a 1-quart baking dish coated with nonstick cooking spray.

2 Combine ¼ cup brown sugar and the flour; cut in 1 tablespoon margarine until mixture is crumbly. Stir in pecans; sprinkle pecan mixture over sweet potato mixture. Bake at 350° for 30 minutes or until mixture is thoroughly heated.

Per ½-cup serving: CALORIES 234 (18% from fat); FAT 4.6g (sat 0.7g, mono 2g, poly 1.7g); PROTEIN 3g; CARBOHYDRATE 46.4g; FIBER 2.2g; CHOLESTEROL 0mg; IRON 2mg; SODIUM 262mg; CALCIUM 59mg

---

FYI

Canned mashed sweet potatoes can be used interchangeably with yams. You'll find both in the canned vegetable section of your supermarket.

Cranberry Scones

8 scones

prep: 12 minutes   cook: 20 minutes

1½ cups all-purpose flour
½ teaspoon baking soda
¼ teaspoon salt
2 tablespoons sugar
1 teaspoon cream of tartar
3 tablespoons stick margarine, chilled
    and cut into pieces
⅔ cup sweetened dried cranberries
2 teaspoons grated orange rind
¾ cup nonfat buttermilk

1 tablespoon all-purpose flour
Nonstick cooking spray
2 teaspoons sugar

1 Preheat the oven to 375°. Combine first 5 ingredients in a large bowl; cut in margarine with a pastry blender or 2 forks until mixture resembles coarse meal. Stir in cranberries and orange rind, tossing well. Add buttermilk to dry ingredients, stirring just until dry ingredients are moistened.

2 Sprinkle 1 tablespoon flour evenly over work surface. Turn dough out onto floured surface; knead 4 or 5 times. Divide dough into 2 portions. Pat each portion into a 5" circle on a baking sheet coated with nonstick cooking spray. Cut each circle into 4 wedges, cutting to, but not through, bottom of dough. Sprinkle each circle evenly with 1 teaspoon sugar. Bake at 375° for 20 minutes or until golden.

Per scone: CALORIES 184 (23% from fat); FAT 4.6g (sat 0.8g, mono 2.5g, poly 1.1g); PROTEIN 3.4g; CARBOHYDRATE 32.8g; FIBER 1.3g; CHOLESTEROL 0mg; IRON 1.2mg; SODIUM 225mg; CALCIUM 35mg

Scone Savvy

Scones are best served right out of the oven—so have the gang ready! We used dried cranberries in these scones, so you'll be able to enjoy the sweet-tart taste year-round.

Blueberry Coffee Cake

8 servings

prep: 10 minutes   cook: 20 minutes

½ cup whole grain yellow cornmeal
¼ cup plus 2 tablespoons all-purpose flour
1 teaspoon baking powder
¼ teaspoon salt
¼ cup plus 2 tablespoons granulated sugar, divided

½ cup nonfat buttermilk
¼ cup fat-free egg substitute
1 tablespoon vegetable oil
1 teaspoon vanilla extract
Nonstick cooking spray
1½ cups fresh or frozen blueberries

½ teaspoon ground cinnamon
1 teaspoon powdered sugar

1 Preheat the oven to 425°. Combine cornmeal, flour, baking powder, salt, and ¼ cup granulated sugar in a large bowl; make a well in center of mixture.

2 Combine buttermilk and next 3 ingredients; add to dry ingredients, stirring just until dry ingredients are moistened. Pour batter into an 8" round cakepan coated with nonstick cooking spray. Top with blueberries.

3 Combine remaining 2 tablespoons granulated sugar and the cinnamon; sprinkle evenly over blueberries. Bake at 425° for 20 minutes or until a wooden toothpick inserted in center comes out clean. Cool 10 minutes in pan on a wire rack; sift powdered sugar evenly over cake. Serve warm.

Per serving: CALORIES 129 (15% from fat); FAT 2.2g (sat 0.2g, mono 0.8g, poly 0.9g); PROTEIN 2.7g; CARBOHYDRATE 25.3g; FIBER 1.5g; CHOLESTEROL 0mg; IRON 0.9mg; SODIUM 168mg; CALCIUM 60mg

A Grain of Knowledge

Whole grain cornmeal is sweeter than the regular kind and adds an earthy flavor to this tender cake layer. If you can't find "whole grain" on the label, look for "stone ground"—which is always whole grain.

Mexican Chocolate Cake

8 servings

prep: 10 minutes   cook: 25 minutes

1	cup all-purpose flour
¾	teaspoon baking powder
½	teaspoon baking soda
½	teaspoon salt
½	cup packed dark brown sugar
¼	cup unsweetened cocoa
½	teaspoon ground cinnamon
⅛	teaspoon ground red pepper
1	cup nonfat buttermilk
¼	cup fat-free egg substitute
1	tablespoon vegetable oil

Nonstick cooking spray
2   tablespoons finely chopped slivered almonds, toasted (see tip on page 41)

1 Preheat the oven to 375°. Combine first 8 ingredients in a medium bowl; make a well in center of mixture.

2 Combine buttermilk, egg substitute, and oil; add to dry ingredients, stirring just until dry ingredients are moistened.

3 Pour batter into an 8" round cakepan coated with nonstick cooking spray. Sprinkle with almonds.

4 Bake at 375° for 25 minutes or until a wooden toothpick inserted in center comes out clean. Cool 10 minutes in pan on a wire rack. Serve warm.

Per serving: CALORIES 156 (18% from fat); FAT 3.1g (sat 0.5g, mono 1.4g, poly 1g); PROTEIN 4.4g; CARBOHYDRATE 29g; FIBER 1.6g; CHOLESTEROL 0mg; IRON 1.7mg; SODIUM 322mg; CALCIUM 89mg

❝*No, it's not a misprint—there really is ground red pepper in this cake! I use a pinch of it to bring out the chocolate and cinnamon flavors that are traditional in Mexican chocolate desserts.*❞

Chocolate Chip Cookies

about 4 dozen

prep: about 23 minutes   cook: 10 minutes per batch

2⅓ cups all-purpose flour
½   teaspoon baking soda

1   cup packed brown sugar
¾   cup stick margarine, softened
½   cup granulated sugar
½   cup fat-free egg substitute
2   teaspoons vanilla extract
1¼ cups semisweet mini chocolate chips

1 Preheat the oven to 350°. Combine flour and baking soda in a large bowl; set aside.

2 Beat brown sugar, margarine, and granulated sugar at medium speed of an electric beater until blended. Add egg substitute and vanilla, beating well. Gradually add flour mixture, beating well. Stir in chocolate chips.

3 Drop dough by rounded tablespoonfuls onto ungreased baking sheets. Bake at 350° for 10 minutes or until golden. Remove cookies from baking sheets, and cool completely on wire racks.

Sh-h-h! Mini chips are my secret to guaranteeing you a chocolate chip in every bite of these cookies! Ooh they're so good—and better for you!

Per cookie: CALORIES 95 (40% from fat); FAT 4.2g (sat 1.3g, mono 1.8g, poly 0.9g); PROTEIN 1.1g; CARBOHYDRATE 14.1g; FIBER 0.4g; CHOLESTEROL 0mg; IRON 0.6mg; SODIUM 44mg; CALCIUM 7mg

Easy Entrées

❝Let my fast and easy entrées be your guide to hassle-free meal planning.❞

Catfish Meunière

4 servings

prep: 5 minutes   cook: 12 minutes

1   large egg, lightly beaten
¼   cup milk
½   cup all-purpose flour
½   teaspoon salt
½   teaspoon ground red pepper
4   farm-raised catfish fillets (about 1½
      to 2 pounds)

½   cup butter, divided
¼   cup vegetable oil

2   tablespoons chopped fresh parsley
      or 2 teaspoons dried parsley
2   tablespoons lemon juice
½   teaspoon Worcestershire sauce

1 Combine egg and milk in a large shallow bowl. Combine flour, salt, and pepper in a shallow dish. Dip fish in egg mixture, and dredge in flour mixture.

2 Melt ¼ cup butter in a large nonstick skillet over medium heat. Add oil; increase heat to medium-high. Place fish in skillet, and cook 4 minutes on each side or until fish flakes easily with a fork. Drain on paper towels.

3 Melt remaining ¼ cup butter in skillet; stir in chopped parsley, lemon juice, and Worcestershire sauce. Spoon over fish.

"Meunière *is a fancy French term for fish that's lightly seasoned, dusted with flour, and pan-fried. You might just like to call this fried catfish!"*

Grouper with Pecan Sauce

4 servings

prep: 6 minutes   cook: 28 minutes

4   grouper or flounder fillets (1½ to 2 pounds)
1   tablespoon soy sauce

¼   cup all-purpose flour
3   tablespoons vegetable oil

1   cup whipping cream
1   tablespoon dark corn syrup or molasses
1   teaspoon soy sauce
½   cup pecan pieces, toasted

1 Place fish in a shallow dish. Brush with 1 tablespoon soy sauce; cover and chill 10 minutes.

2 Place flour in another shallow dish; dredge fish in flour, shaking off excess flour. Heat oil in a large nonstick skillet over medium-high heat. Add fish; cook 6 to 8 minutes on each side or until fish is golden and flakes easily with a fork. Remove fish from skillet, and keep warm.

3 Wipe skillet dry with a paper towel. Add whipping cream and corn syrup to skillet; bring to a boil over medium heat. Boil until mixture is reduced to ¾ cup (about 5 minutes). Stir in 1 teaspoon soy sauce and pecans; spoon sauce over fish.

Be Selective
Fish should have a clean, mild aroma—not an offensive fishy or ammonia odor. The fish should be firm and elastic. Gills should be pinkish red and not slippery; the eyes should be clear, clean, and full.

Grilled Herbed Salmon

(pictured on facing page)

8 servings

prep: 10 minutes   cook: 8 minutes

Nonstick cooking spray
⅓   cup dry white wine
⅓   cup olive oil
2   teaspoons chopped fresh thyme
2   teaspoons chopped fresh marjoram
2   teaspoons chopped fresh sage
2   teaspoons chopped fresh parsley
2   teaspoons lemon juice
½   teaspoon salt
⅛   teaspoon freshly ground pepper

8   (6-ounce) salmon fillets

1 Spray cold grill rack with nonstick cooking spray. Preheat the grill to medium-high heat (350° to 400°). Combine white wine and next 8 ingredients in a small jar; cover tightly, and shake vigorously.

2 Coat fish with cooking spray before placing on grill. Grill fish, skin side down and covered, 7 to 8 minutes or until fish flakes easily with a fork; baste with herb mixture and turn once.

Note: Substitute ¾ teaspoon each of dried thyme, marjoram, rubbed sage, and parsley flakes for the fresh herbs listed at left, if desired.

Heart-Healthy Salmon
Not only is salmon good, it's good for you! Eating salmon may reduce the risk of heart disease, due to high amounts of polyunsaturated omega-3 fatty acids.

Mini BBQ Meat Loaves,
Garlic Mashed Potatoes,
and steamed green beans,
pages 85 and 94

Chicken-Sausage Gumbo,
page 134

Honey-Ginger Chicken Kabobs

(pictured on facing page)

4 servings

prep: 20 minutes   cook: 12 minutes

Nonstick cooking spray
1½ pounds skinned and boned chicken
     breasts, cut into 1" pieces
½   teaspoon salt
½   teaspoon black pepper
1   yellow bell pepper, seeded and cut
     into 1½" pieces
1   red bell pepper, seeded and cut into
     1½" pieces

⅓   cup hoisin sauce
⅓   cup honey
½   teaspoon minced fresh ginger or
     ⅛ teaspoon ground ginger
1   clove garlic, minced

1 Spray cold grill rack with nonstick cooking spray. Preheat the grill to medium-high heat (350° to 400°). Sprinkle chicken with salt and black pepper. Thread chicken and bell pepper pieces onto 4 long metal skewers.

2 Combine hoisin sauce and remaining 3 ingredients, stirring well; brush lightly on kabobs. Place kabobs on grill rack; grill, covered, 12 minutes, turning and basting up until the last 4 minutes with hoisin sauce mixture.

No-Stick Solution
The honey in the basting sauce may cause the kabobs
to stick to the grill rack. Just give the loaded skewers
a few sprays of nonstick cooking spray before placing
them on the grill to prevent any sticking.

Buttermilk-Pecan Chicken

8 servings

prep: 15 minutes   cook: 30 minutes

1   cup buttermilk
1   large egg, lightly beaten

1   cup ground pecans (see tip)
¾   cup fine, dry breadcrumbs
      (store-bought)
2   teaspoons paprika
1½ teaspoons salt
⅛   teaspoon pepper

½   cup all-purpose flour
8   skinned and boned chicken breasts

⅓   cup butter, melted
¼   cup coarsely chopped pecans (see tip)

1 Preheat the oven to 350°. Combine buttermilk and egg in a shallow dish.

2 Combine ground pecans and next 4 ingredients in another shallow dish.

3 Place flour in a third shallow dish; dredge chicken in flour. Dip in buttermilk mixture; drain. Dredge chicken in pecan mixture.

4 Place chicken on a lightly greased rack in a broiler pan. Drizzle chicken with melted butter; sprinkle with chopped pecans. Bake, uncovered, at 350° for 30 minutes or until done.

Processing Frenzy

Let your food processor be your new best friend for such jobs as grinding a cup of pecans. It'll also do a good job at coarsely chopping them.

Garlicky Chicken

4 servings

prep: 4 minutes   cook: 20 minutes

½   cup all-purpose flour
4   skinned and boned chicken breasts
¼   cup butter
4   large cloves garlic, minced (see tip)

1   cup apple juice
2   tablespoons lemon juice
½   teaspoon pepper

1 Place flour in a shallow dish; dredge chicken in flour. Melt butter in a large skillet over medium heat; add chicken and garlic. Cook 4 to 5 minutes on each side or until chicken is done. Remove chicken from skillet; keep warm.

2 Add apple juice, lemon juice, and pepper to skillet; bring mixture to a boil. Boil, uncovered, 4 minutes or until reduced to ½ cup. Pour sauce over chicken, and serve immediately.

Fresh Is Best
Mince fresh garlic for optimal flavor in this recipe. The simpler the recipe, the bigger difference fresh ingredients make.

Nacho Chicken

2 servings

prep: 5 minutes   cook: 25 minutes

2   tablespoons mayonnaise
¼   teaspoon salt
¼   teaspoon dried Italian seasoning
2   skinned and boned chicken breasts
¾   cup crushed nacho cheese-flavored
        tortilla chips (about 30)

1   tablespoon butter, melted

1 Preheat the oven to 350°. Combine first 3 ingredients; spread on both sides of chicken. Place crushed chips in a shallow dish; dredge chicken in chips.

2 Place chicken on a lightly greased baking sheet. Drizzle with butter. Bake at 350° for 20 to 25 minutes or until chicken is done.

“My secret to the crispy coating in this simple chicken dish is the tasty nacho cheese chips. But don't worry—I'll leave you enough chips to snack on!”

Crescent Chicken Squares

4 servings

prep: 15 minutes   cook: 25 minutes

1   (3-ounce) package cream cheese,
     softened
3   tablespoons butter, melted and
     divided
2   cups chopped cooked chicken
2   tablespoons milk
¼   teaspoon salt
⅛   teaspoon pepper

1   (8-ounce) can refrigerated crescent
     rolls

¾   cup seasoned croutons, crushed

1 Preheat the oven to 350°. Combine cream cheese and 2 tablespoons butter; stir in chicken and next 3 ingredients. Set aside.

2 Unroll crescent dough, separating into 4 rectangles; press perforations to seal. Spoon ¼ of chicken mixture into center of each rectangle; bring corners of each rectangle together over chicken mixture, and twist gently to seal.

3 Brush packets with remaining 1 tablespoon melted butter; dredge in crushed croutons, and place on an ungreased baking sheet. Bake, uncovered, at 350° for 20 to 25 minutes or until golden.

Go for the Gravy
Dress up these cheesy crescents with a drizzle of warm gravy. It's so easy when you use the convenient heat-and-serve kind.

Creamy Chicken Divine

6 servings

prep: 5 minutes   cook: 18 minutes

2   (10-ounce) packages frozen broccoli
      spears

1   (10¾-ounce) can cream of chicken
      soup, undiluted
3   cups chopped cooked chicken
¼   teaspoon poultry seasoning
1   (8-ounce) container sour cream
1   cup (4 ounces) shredded Cheddar
      cheese

16   round buttery crackers, crushed
      (about ¾ cup)
2   tablespoons slivered almonds
1½ tablespoons butter, melted

1 Place broccoli in a shallow 2-quart microwave-safe baking dish. Cover tightly with heavy-duty plastic wrap; fold back a small corner of wrap to allow steam to escape. Microwave at HIGH 7 minutes; drain and set aside.

2 Combine soup, chicken, and poultry seasoning in a microwave-safe bowl; cover and microwave at HIGH 3 minutes. Stir in sour cream and ½ cup shredded cheese. Microwave, uncovered, at HIGH 2 minutes. Spoon chicken mixture over broccoli; sprinkle with remaining cheese.

3 Combine cracker crumbs, almonds, and butter; sprinkle over cheese. Microwave, uncovered, at HIGH 6 minutes.

Note: This recipe was tested in an 1100-watt microwave oven.

"Thanks to the microwave, this classic chicken divan is done in 18 minutes—making it divine in my book!"

Steak in Pepper Cream

2 to 4 servings

prep: 3 minutes   cook: 20 minutes

¼   teaspoon salt
2   (12-ounce) New York strip steaks
        (¾" thick)

1½ tablespoons green peppercorns in
        liquid, drained (see tip)
2   tablespoons steak sauce
2   tablespoons water

1   cup whipping cream
¼   teaspoon ground black pepper

1 Place a 10" cast-iron skillet over
medium heat until hot; sprinkle salt
in skillet. Place steaks over salt; cook
4 minutes on each side or until browned.
Remove from skillet.

2 Combine peppercorns, steak sauce,
and water in hot skillet; cook over
medium heat, stirring constantly, to
loosen any browned bits in bottom
of skillet.

3 Stir in whipping cream and black
pepper. Bring to a boil; reduce heat,
and simmer, stirring constantly, 3 to 4
minutes or until slightly thickened. Add
steaks; simmer 5 minutes or to desired
doneness, stirring occasionally.

Pick a Peck of Peppercorns
Peppercorns are available in 3 varieties that are
harvested at different stages of maturity—black,
green, and white. Look for them in small jars on
the grocery shelf near the pickles.

Easy Spaghetti

(pictured on cover)

4 to 6 servings

prep: 5 minutes   cook: 25 minutes

8   to 12 ounces uncooked spaghetti

1   pound ground beef
1   small onion, chopped

2   (14½-ounce) cans Italian-style diced
       tomatoes, undrained
2   (6-ounce) cans tomato paste
½   cup water
2   teaspoons dried Italian seasoning
2   teaspoons sugar
Shredded Parmesan cheese (optional)

1 Cook pasta according to package directions; keep warm.

2 Meanwhile, cook beef and onion in a large skillet over medium-high heat, stirring until the beef crumbles and is no longer pink; drain.

3 Stir in diced tomatoes and next 4 ingredients. Cook over medium heat, about 20 minutes, stirring occasionally. Serve over warm cooked pasta. Sprinkle with Parmesan cheese, if desired.

If You've Got the Time...
Prefer a spaghetti sauce that has simmered all day? Try this recipe in a slow cooker: Cook ground beef and onion as directed on the cooktop. Add remaining ingredients except spaghetti; spoon into an electric slow cooker. Cook on LOW 6 to 7 hours or on HIGH 3 to 4 hours.

Beef-Stuffed Peppers

4 servings

prep: 11 minutes   cook: 13 minutes

4   medium-sized green bell peppers

1   large egg, lightly beaten
1   (14-ounce) jar spaghetti sauce,
        divided
1   cup seasoned croutons, crushed
1   teaspoon dried onion flakes or
        ½ teaspoon onion powder
¼   teaspoon black pepper
¾   pound ground round

Grated Parmesan cheese

❝I prefer ground round for this recipe. It's lean enough to stuff into the bell peppers without cooking and draining it first, which is a big time-saver!❞

1 Cut off tops of bell peppers, and remove seeds and membranes.

2 Combine egg, ¾ cup spaghetti sauce, and next 4 ingredients. Stuff peppers with beef mixture; place peppers in a lightly greased 8" square microwave-safe baking dish. Cover loosely with wax paper.

3 Microwave at HIGH 12 minutes, giving dish a half-turn after 6 minutes if your microwave doesn't have a turntable. Spoon 1 tablespoon spaghetti sauce over each pepper; sprinkle with Parmesan cheese, and microwave at HIGH 45 seconds. Heat remaining spaghetti sauce, and serve with bell peppers.

Note: This recipe was tested in an 1100-watt microwave oven.

Green Chili Enchiladas

4 servings

prep: 15 minutes   cook: 32 minutes

1½ pounds ground chuck
1   small onion, chopped
1   (10¾-ounce) can cream of
     mushroom soup, undiluted
2   (4.5-ounce) cans chopped green
     chilies, undrained and divided

8   (8" or 9") flour tortillas
1   (8-ounce) package shredded
     colby-Monterey Jack cheese blend
1   (10¾-ounce) can Cheddar cheese
     soup, undiluted

Salsa

1 Preheat the oven to 350°. Cook beef and onion in a large skillet over medium-high heat, stirring until the beef crumbles and is no longer pink; drain. Stir in mushroom soup and 1 can green chilies.

2 Spoon about ½ cup beef mixture down center of each tortilla; sprinkle each with 2½ tablespoons shredded cheese. Roll up tortillas; place seam side down in a lightly greased 9" x 13" baking dish. Stir remaining 1 can green chilies into Cheddar soup. Spoon mixture over tortillas, spreading to edges. Sprinkle remaining shredded cheese over enchiladas.

3 Cover and bake at 350° for 20 minutes; uncover and bake 5 more minutes. Serve with salsa.

"Plan a fiesta with your gang by putting these enchiladas on the menu. They're loaded with cheese, making them an instant favorite with the kiddies!"

Teriyaki Hamburgers

4 servings

prep: 5 minutes   cook: 20 minutes

1½ pounds ground beef
3   tablespoons teriyaki or soy sauce
1   tablespoon honey
1   teaspoon salt
¾   teaspoon ground ginger
2   cloves garlic, minced

4   hamburger buns, toasted
Lettuce leaves
Tomato slices

1 Combine first 6 ingredients; shape into 4 patties. Cook patties in a large skillet over medium-low heat 20 minutes, turning once.

2 Place patties on bottoms of buns; top with lettuce, tomatoes, desired condiments, and tops of buns.

66Spread a little Chinese mustard on these burgers for a tangy surprise!99

Beef Fajita Pizza

(pictured on page 2)

4 servings

prep: 10 minutes   cook: 23 minutes

2   teaspoons chili powder
¼   teaspoon garlic powder
½   pound lean, boneless sirloin steak,
     trimmed

1   small green bell pepper, cut into
     strips
½   medium-sized red onion, thinly
     sliced and separated into rings
1   (14-ounce) package prebaked Italian
     pizza bread shell
½   cup chunky salsa
1   cup (4 ounces) shredded Cheddar
     cheese

1 Preheat the oven to 450°. Heat a nonstick skillet over medium-high heat. While skillet heats, combine chili powder and garlic powder in a small bowl; sprinkle over both sides of steak. Add steak to skillet; cook 5 minutes on each side. Remove steak from skillet; let stand 6 to 8 minutes. Slice steak diagonally across grain into ¼" slices.

2 While steak stands, arrange pepper strips and onion on bread shell. Arrange steak strips over vegetables. Spoon salsa over steak. Bake at 450° for 8 minutes; sprinkle with cheese. Bake 5 more minutes.

❝Enjoy the flavors of a fajita atop a pizza! If you haven't tried prepared pizza bread shells yet, then do so. They're flavorful and save lots of time on the crust.❞

Mushroom-Veal Marsala

4 servings

prep: 6 minutes   cook: 13 minutes

1   teaspoon chopped fresh or dried
    rosemary
½   teaspoon salt
½   teaspoon freshly ground pepper
1   pound veal scaloppine (¼" thick)
2   tablespoons olive oil

1   (8-ounce) package sliced fresh
    mushrooms
2   cloves garlic, minced

2   teaspoons cornstarch
1   teaspoon chicken bouillon granules
⅔   cup water
⅓   cup dry Marsala (see tip)

1 Rub first 3 ingredients over veal. Heat oil in a large nonstick skillet over medium heat. Add half of veal; cook 2 minutes on each side or until light golden. Remove veal from skillet; keep warm. Repeat with remaining veal.

2 Add mushrooms and garlic to empty skillet; cook over medium-high heat, stirring constantly, 3 minutes or until tender.

3 Combine cornstarch and remaining 3 ingredients; add to skillet. Cook, stirring constantly, 1 minute or until thick and bubbly. Serve over veal.

A Splash of Vino
Marsala is a smoky-flavored Italian wine. You can substitute ⅓ cup dry white wine plus 1 teaspoon brandy for Marsala, or simply use ⅓ cup white grape juice.

Garlicky Mustard Lamb Chops

4 servings

prep: 7 minutes   cook: 14 minutes

2	cloves garlic, minced
½	teaspoon pepper
¼	teaspoon dried thyme
⅛	teaspoon salt
2	teaspoons lemon juice
2	teaspoons Dijon mustard
1	teaspoon olive oil
4	(5-ounce) lean lamb loin chops

1 Preheat the broiler. Combine garlic, pepper, thyme, and salt in a small bowl; mash with back of a spoon until mixture forms a paste. Stir in lemon juice, mustard, and olive oil.

2 Trim fat from lamb chops. Spread garlic mixture over both sides of chops. Place chops on a lightly greased rack in a broiler pan. Broil 6 to 7 minutes on each side or to desired degree of doneness.

Savvy Substitute

This rub will enhance pork chops just as well. Substitute 4 (5-ounce) pork chops for the lamb, if desired.

Peachy Pork Chops

4 servings

prep: 5 minutes   cook: 24 minutes

4   (1"-thick) pork chops
¼   teaspoon seasoned salt
¼   teaspoon onion powder

1   (16-ounce) can peach slices,
        undrained
2   tablespoons brown sugar
2   tablespoons butter
½   teaspoon dried basil

1 Preheat the broiler. Place pork chops on a lightly greased rack in a broiler pan. Sprinkle with salt and onion powder. Broil 5½" from heat 7 minutes on each side or to desired doneness.

2 Combine peaches and remaining 3 ingredients in a saucepan. Cook, uncovered, over low heat 10 minutes, stirring often. Arrange chops on a platter. Pour peach sauce over chops.

66*You don't have to wait till peaches are in season to enjoy these chops. Canned peaches work nicely, making it a real peach of a dish!***99**

Fiesta Quesadillas

4 to 6 servings

prep: 19 minutes   cook: 6 minutes

1½ cups diced cooked ham
3   plum tomatoes, seeded and
     chopped
1   cup crumbled goat cheese
½   medium-sized red onion, diced
¼   cup chopped fresh cilantro
¼   cup lime juice
¼   cup (2 ounces) cream cheese,
     softened
1   (4.5-ounce) can chopped green
     chilies, drained
6   (8") flour tortillas

Nonstick cooking spray

1 Combine first 8 ingredients. Spread 1 side of each tortilla with about ½ cup ham mixture; fold tortillas in half.

2 Coat a large nonstick skillet with nonstick cooking spray, and place over medium-high heat. Add tortillas, and cook, in batches, 1 minute on each side or until golden. Serve immediately.

❝Quesadillas go fancy schmancy here, thanks to goat cheese. Don't forget the margaritas for a true fiesta!❞

Just Peachy Glazed Ham

3 to 4 servings

prep: 5 minutes   cook: 11 minutes

1   (16-ounce) can peach slices in light
      syrup, undrained

2   tablespoons dark brown sugar
2   to 3 teaspoons Dijon mustard

1   (1-pound) center-cut ham slice
⅓   cup sliced scallions

1 Drain peaches, reserving ½ cup syrup in a large skillet; set peaches aside.

2 Add sugar and mustard to skillet; bring to a boil over medium-high heat. Cook 2 minutes or until mixture is slightly reduced.

3 Add ham, and cook 2 minutes on each side. Add peaches and scallions; cover and cook over low heat 3 minutes or until peaches are thoroughly heated.

Ham steak is the perfect quick weeknight meal. It heats faster than a whole ham, and nothing goes to waste!

Easy Crab Bake

4 servings

prep: 15 minutes   cook: 30 minutes

1   large egg, lightly beaten
¾   cup mayonnaise
2   tablespoons lemon juice
1½   teaspoons hot sauce
¼   teaspoon salt
1   pound fresh crabmeat, drained and
     flaked

¼   cup fine, dry breadcrumbs
     (store-bought)
1   tablespoon butter, melted

1 Preheat the oven to 325°. Combine first 5 ingredients; stir well. Pick through crabmeat to remove any bits of shell and cartilage. Fold crabmeat into egg mixture. Spoon mixture into a lightly greased 1-quart baking dish.

2 Combine breadcrumbs and butter; sprinkle over crabmeat mixture. Bake, uncovered, at 325° for 25 to 30 minutes. Serve with lemon wedges, if desired.

❝Most of the prep time is spent picking through the crabmeat to remove any bits of shell and cartilage. Don't let that deter you, 'cause the end results are well worth the effort! So be happy—not crabby!❞

Scallops in Vermouth Cream

2 servings

prep: 4 minutes   cook: 10 minutes

2   tablespoons all-purpose flour
1   pound sea scallops
2   tablespoons butter

¼   cup dry vermouth or other white
       wine (see tip)
½   cup whipping cream
¼   teaspoon salt
⅛   teaspoon pepper

1 Place flour in a shallow dish; toss scallops in flour. Melt butter in a large skillet over medium heat; add scallops. Cook 4 to 5 minutes or until scallops turn white throughout and are golden on both sides, turning occasionally. Remove scallops from skillet.

2 Add vermouth to skillet, stirring to loosen bits from bottom of skillet; bring to a boil. Cook 2 minutes or until vermouth is reduced by half. Stir in whipping cream, salt, and pepper; reduce heat to low. Add scallops; cook just until thoroughly heated.

Rich in Flavor
Vermouth is a white wine that's flavored with herbs and spices. Save this recipe for when you want to whip up something special for two! Add some crusty bread or rice to soak up this rich vermouth cream.

Spicy Louisiana-Style Shrimp

6 servings

prep: 5 minutes   cook: 20 minutes

1   (16-ounce) loaf French bread, cut in
     half lengthwise

1   cup butter
2   onions, chopped
1½   teaspoons minced garlic
1   teaspoon Creole seasoning

3   pounds unpeeled, large fresh
     shrimp, peeled and deveined
     (see tip)

1 Preheat the oven to 350°. Place French bread halves cut side up on a baking sheet. Bake at 350° for 5 minutes or until bread is golden. Cut each bread half into 3 pieces, and set aside.

2 Melt butter in a Dutch oven. Add onions, garlic, and seasoning. Cook over medium heat until onions are tender.

3 Add shrimp. Cover and cook 8 minutes or until shrimp turn pink. Serve over bread.

Time-saver

If time's a factor, buy already peeled shrimp at the supermarket. You'll need 2¼ pounds of peeled, large fresh shrimp to equal 3 pounds of large fresh shrimp in the shell.

Pecan-Crusted Salmon

4 servings

prep: 5 minutes   cook: 15 minutes

4   salmon fillets
¼   teaspoon salt
⅛   teaspoon pepper

2   tablespoons Dijon mustard
2   tablespoons butter, melted
1½ tablespoons honey
¼   cup soft breadcrumbs (homemade)
¼   cup finely chopped pecans
1   tablespoon chopped fresh parsley

1 Preheat the oven to 450°. Sprinkle fish with salt and pepper; place skin side down in a lightly greased 7" x 11" or 9" square baking dish.

2 Combine mustard, butter, and honey in a small bowl; brush over fish. Combine breadcrumbs, pecans, and parsley in another small bowl; spoon evenly across top of fish.

3 Bake, uncovered, at 450° for 12 to 15 minutes or until fish flakes easily with a fork.

66*Try this crunchy pecan coating on grouper or other white fish fillets—it'll be equally delicious!*99

Grilled Caribbean Tuna

4 servings

prep: 3 minutes   cook: 8 minutes

½   cup mayonnaise
1   tablespoon lime juice
½   teaspoon ground red pepper
½   teaspoon ground cumin
1   clove garlic, crushed

4   tuna steaks

1 Preheat the grill to medium heat (300° to 350°). Combine first 5 ingredients in a medium bowl.

2 Brush mayonnaise mixture on both sides of fish. Grill fish, covered, 3 to 4 minutes on each side or until fish flakes easily with a fork.

In just about 10 minutes, you can have flavor-packed grilled tuna steaks on the table for the family. Now, that's what I call quick and easy!

Soup, Salad & Sandwich Sensations

"Have we got a super selection of salads, sandwiches—and, yes—soups for you! Some stand on their own as meals while others might be paired with recipes within this chapter. You won't be disappointed either way!"

Corn Chowder

3 servings

prep: 10 minutes   cook: 33 minutes

6   slices bacon

1   cup chopped onion
2   medium-sized round red potatoes,
        cubed
½   cup water

1   (14.75-ounce) can cream-style corn
1½ cups half-and-half
½   teaspoon salt
Dash of pepper

1 Cook bacon in a Dutch oven until crisp; remove bacon, reserving 2 tablespoons drippings in Dutch oven. Crumble bacon, and set aside.

2 Cook onion in drippings over medium heat, stirring constantly, until tender. Add potatoes and water; bring to a boil. Cover, reduce heat, and simmer 18 minutes or until potatoes are tender.

3 Stir corn and remaining 3 ingredients into potato mixture; cook until thoroughly heated, stirring often. Ladle into bowls, and sprinkle with bacon.

Mexican Cornsticks

Try these cornsticks with any of the soups in this chapter.

Combine 1¼ cups all-purpose flour, ¾ cup yellow cornmeal, 2 teaspoons baking powder, 1 teaspoon baking soda, ½ teaspoon salt, and ⅛ teaspoon ground red pepper in a medium bowl; make a well in center of mixture. Combine ¾ cup buttermilk, 8¾-ounce can cream-style corn, 4.5-ounce can chopped green chilies, 1 large egg, and ½ cup (2 ounces) shredded sharp Cheddar cheese in a large bowl. Add to flour mixture, stirring until moistened. Spoon into lightly greased cornstick pans, filling two-thirds full. Bake at 425° for 18 to 20 minutes or until golden. Remove from pans immediately. Yield: 16 cornsticks.

Creamy Chicken 'n' Vegetable Chowder

about 5 servings

prep: 5 minutes   cook: 15 minutes

1   (11-ounce) can Mexican-style corn, undrained
1   (10¾-ounce) can cream of chicken soup, undiluted
1   (10¾-ounce) can cream of potato soup, undiluted
1   (4.5-ounce) jar sliced mushrooms, undrained
1   (4.5-ounce) can chopped green chilies, undrained
2   cups chopped cooked chicken (see tip)
1½ cups milk
1   cup chicken broth
⅓   cup sliced scallions

1½ cups (6 ounces) shredded Cheddar cheese

1 Combine first 9 ingredients in a Dutch oven; cook over medium heat 15 minutes or until mixture is thoroughly heated, stirring occasionally.

2 Remove Dutch oven from heat; add cheese to chowder, stirring until cheese melts.

❝ Chowder can't get much easier than with this recipe that's loaded with convenience products and lots of flavor! Check out the rotisserie chickens in the deli section of your supermarket. Generally, 1 whole rotisserie chicken gives you 3 cups of chopped cooked chicken.❞

Chicken-Sausage Gumbo

(pictured on page 107)

4 to 6 servings

prep: 18 minutes   cook: 28 minutes

½   pound smoked sausage, cut into
      ¼" slices

1   to 3 tablespoons vegetable oil
5   tablespoons all-purpose flour

1   cup coarsely chopped onion
1   cup chopped celery
2   large cloves garlic, pressed
1   medium-sized green bell pepper,
      chopped
2   cups chicken broth
1   (28-ounce) can diced tomatoes
1   to 2 teaspoons Creole seasoning
4   cups chopped cooked chicken
Warm cooked rice

1 Cook sausage over medium-high heat in a Dutch oven 3 minutes, stirring often. Remove sausage with a slotted spoon. Drain.

2 Add enough oil to drippings in Dutch oven to equal 3 tablespoons; whisk in flour, and cook over medium-high heat, whisking constantly, 5 minutes.

3 Add onion and next 3 ingredients; cook 5 minutes, stirring often. Stir in broth, tomatoes, and Creole seasoning. Bring to a boil; cover, reduce heat, and simmer 5 minutes. Add sausage and chicken; simmer, covered, 5 minutes. Serve over warm cooked rice.

"My streamlined version of gumbo is sure to please even the strictest of gumbo aficionados. Try it, and see for yourself!"

Quick Chili Mole

6 servings

prep: 8 minutes   cook: 25 minutes

1   pound ground chuck
1   medium onion, chopped
1   clove garlic, minced

3   (8-ounce) cans tomato sauce
1   tablespoon chili powder
1   milk chocolate kiss
1   (15-ounce) can kidney beans,
        undrained
Toppings: shredded Cheddar cheese,
        sour cream

1 Cook first 3 ingredients in a Dutch oven over medium-high heat until the beef crumbles and is no longer pink; drain.

2 Stir tomato sauce, chili powder, and chocolate kiss into beef mixture. Cook, uncovered, over low heat 15 minutes, stirring occasionally. Add beans, and cook until thoroughly heated. Ladle chili into bowls; top with desired toppings.

Chocolate Chili

Chocolate is a traditional ingredient in mole (pronounced "MOH-lay") that adds a richness to the sauce without being overly sweet. It adds a more authentic Tex-Mex flavor to this chili.

Veggie-Mac Soup

6 to 8 servings

prep: 4 minutes   cook: 25 minutes

3   (14-ounce) cans chicken broth,
      undiluted
1   (16-ounce) package frozen mixed
      vegetables
1   (14½-ounce) can Italian-style stewed
      tomatoes, undrained and chopped
1   (8½-ounce) can whole kernel corn,
      drained
2   tablespoons dried onion flakes
¼   teaspoon pepper
2   cloves garlic, minced

½   cup elbow macaroni, uncooked

1 Combine first 7 ingredients in a Dutch oven; cover and bring to a boil.

2 Stir in pasta; reduce heat, and simmer, uncovered, 20 minutes or until pasta is tender.

66A veggie in every bite—this would make Mama proud! Serve up your gang's favorite combination of mixed veggies in this soup, and there'll be smiles all around.99

White Bean Soup

3 to 4 servings

prep: 9 minutes   cook: 22 minutes

1   (16-ounce) can navy beans,
      undrained (see tip)
1   (15.8-ounce) can great Northern
      beans, undrained
1   cup water

¼   cup butter
2   large carrots, diced
1   cup chopped cooked ham or 1 ham
      hock
⅓   cup chopped scallions
1   bay leaf

1 Combine beans in a large saucepan; mash slightly with a potato masher or back of a large spoon. Stir in water, and cook over low heat until thoroughly heated.

2 Melt butter in a medium skillet over medium-high heat; add carrots, and cook, stirring constantly, until tender. Add carrots, ham, scallions, and bay leaf to bean mixture. Cook over low heat 10 minutes, stirring occasionally. **Remove and discard bay leaf.**

Did You Know?

The navy bean—a type of kidney bean—gets its name from the fact that the U.S. Navy has long considered it a staple on their menus.

Ham-and-Hash Brown Soup

5 servings

prep: 10 minutes   cook: 22 minutes

2½ cups water
2   cups frozen cubed hash brown
         potatoes
2   cups chopped cooked ham
1½ cups thinly sliced carrots
½   cup chopped green bell pepper
¼   cup chopped red bell pepper

1   (14.75-ounce) can cream-style corn
1   (11-ounce) can nacho fiesta cheese
         soup, undiluted
½   cup water
Dash of black pepper

1 Combine first 6 ingredients in a Dutch oven; bring to a boil. Cover, reduce heat, and simmer 15 minutes or until vegetables are tender.

2 Add corn and remaining ingredients to Dutch oven; cook until thoroughly heated, stirring often.

66Supermarkets are making it oh-so-easy to get homecooked meals on the table—fast! Look for already-chopped ham in the meat section and prechopped vegetables with the produce.99

Peppery Potato Soup

2 servings

prep: 7 minutes   cook: 18 minutes

2   cups peeled, cubed potatoes (see tip)
½   cup chopped onion
1   (14-ounce) can chicken broth

1   cup milk
1   teaspoon butter
1   teaspoon chopped fresh thyme or
           ¼ teaspoon dried thyme
¼   teaspoon salt
¼   teaspoon pepper

1 Combine first 3 ingredients in a saucepan. Bring to a boil; cover, reduce heat, and simmer 10 minutes or until potatoes are tender.

2 Remove about 1 cup potatoes from saucepan with a slotted spoon. Mash remaining mixture in saucepan with a potato masher; add reserved potatoes, the milk, and remaining ingredients. Bring to a boil over medium heat, stirring constantly.

Potato Pointers

The best potatoes to use here are baking potatoes, such as russet or Idaho. As they break down in the cooking process, they'll thicken the soup.

Creamy Tomato Soup

3 servings

prep: 5 minutes   cook: 10 minutes

1   (12-ounce) can evaporated milk
1   (10¾-ounce) can tomato soup,
       undiluted
1   (14½-ounce) can Italian-style stewed
       tomatoes, undrained and chopped
½   cup (2 ounces) shredded Cheddar
       cheese

Garlic croutons

1 Combine milk and soup in a medium saucepan; add tomatoes and cheese. Cook over medium-low heat until cheese melts and mixture is thoroughly heated.

2 Ladle soup into bowls, and top with croutons.

"We've taken a simple can of tomato soup and made it into something really special with only 4 other ingredients. Now, that's what I call kitchen genius!"

Mandarin Orange Salad

4 servings

prep: 12 minutes

1 medium head Bibb or Boston
  lettuce, torn
1 (11-ounce) can mandarin oranges,
  chilled and drained
1 ripe avocado, peeled and thinly
  sliced (see tip)
½ cup coarsely chopped pecans,
  toasted
2 scallions, thinly sliced
Freshly ground pepper to taste
⅓ cup Italian salad dressing

1 Combine first 6 ingredients in a salad bowl. Add Italian dressing just before serving, and toss gently.

Just Ripe!

To check the ripeness of an avocado, try to flick the small stem off. If it comes off easily and you can see green underneath, then the avocado is ripe and ready. Rush the ripening of a firm avocado by placing it in a paper bag at room temperature overnight.

Festive Corn Salad

4 servings

prep: 13 minutes

1   (11-ounce) can white whole kernel
       corn, drained and rinsed

1   medium-sized green bell pepper,
       seeded and chopped

1   medium tomato, chopped

1   medium-sized red onion, chopped

¼   teaspoon black pepper

½   cup Italian salad dressing

Lettuce leaves

1 Combine first 6 ingredients; cover and chill, if desired.

2 Spoon corn mixture into a bowl lined with lettuce leaves. Serve with a slotted spoon.

“The colorful vegetables make this salad festive! And when food is pleasin' to the eye, it's especially pleasin' to the palate.”

Tomato-Basil-Mozzarella Salad

(pictured on page 174)

6 servings

prep: 9 minutes   chill: 1 hour

3   large ripe tomatoes, cut into
      ½" slices (about 1½ pounds)
      (see tip)
12 fresh basil leaves
8   ounces mozzarella cheese, cut into
      ¼" strips

1½ tablespoons olive oil
1½ tablespoons lemon juice
¼   teaspoon salt
¼   teaspoon freshly ground pepper

1 Arrange tomato slices on a serving platter. Top each tomato slice with a basil leaf and a cheese strip.

2 Combine oil and lemon juice; drizzle over tomato salad. Sprinkle with salt and pepper. Cover and chill at least 1 hour.

Fresh Is Best
Vine-ripened tomatoes are preferable for this fresh salad. They're available year-round but are at their peak from June through September.

Beefy Blue Salad

4 servings

prep: 10 minutes

8   ounces thinly sliced roast beef

1   pint cherry tomatoes
1   (8½-ounce) package mixed salad
      greens
¼   cup (1 ounce) crumbled blue cheese
      (see tip)
¼   cup olive oil vinaigrette
Parmesan Toasts

1 Arrange roast beef slices into 2 stacks; roll up stacks. Cut into 1" slices.

2 Arrange beef and tomatoes over salad greens. Sprinkle with blue cheese, and drizzle with olive oil vinaigrette. Serve with Parmesan Toasts.

Parmesan Toasts

prep: 7 minutes   cook: 3 minutes

4   Italian bread slices
1   tablespoon butter, melted
¼   cup grated Parmesan cheese
¼   teaspoon freshly ground pepper

1 Preheat the broiler. Brush each bread slice evenly with butter. Sprinkle evenly with cheese and pepper. Place on a baking sheet.

2 Broil 3½" from heat 3 minutes or until light golden.

66_Equal amounts of crumbled feta cheese works just as well as blue cheese with this roast beef salad. Use whichever you like best!_**99**

Asian Pasta Salad

4 servings

prep: 10 minutes   cook: 8 minutes

8	ounces dried linguine, uncooked
3	cups broccoli florets
12	cherry tomatoes, halved
4	scallions, sliced
2	large carrots, scraped and sliced diagonally
¼	cup soy sauce
2	tablespoons sesame seeds, toasted
2	tablespoons brown sugar
2	tablespoons dark sesame oil (see note)
1	tablespoon lemon juice
¼	teaspoon hot sauce
1	large clove garlic, minced

1 Cook pasta according to package directions; drain. Rinse with cold water; drain again. Place pasta in a large bowl. Add broccoli and next 3 ingredients; toss well.

2 Combine soy sauce and remaining 6 ingredients in a small jar; cover tightly, and shake vigorously. Pour over pasta mixture; toss gently.

Note: Look for dark sesame oil in the Asian section of large supermarkets.

Make It Main Dish

Just add chopped cooked chicken, and you've turned this colorful high-flavored mix into a great main-dish salad.

Chicken Caesar Salad

4 servings

prep: 10 minutes   cook: 6 minutes

¼   cup white wine vinegar
2   teaspoons Dijon mustard
1   teaspoon Worcestershire sauce

2   tablespoons lemon-pepper
        seasoning
2   teaspoons garlic powder
1½   pounds chicken breast strips
¼   cup olive oil

1   medium head romaine lettuce, torn
        or shredded (about 8 cups)
2   cups garlic croutons
½   cup shredded Parmesan cheese

1 Combine first 3 ingredients in a small bowl, stirring well; set aside.

2 Place lemon-pepper seasoning and garlic powder in a shallow dish; dredge chicken in seasoning mixture. Heat oil in a large skillet over medium-high heat. Cook chicken in hot oil 5 minutes or until done, turning once. Remove chicken from skillet, reserving drippings in skillet; drain chicken on paper towels.

3 Remove skillet from heat; stir vinegar mixture into reserved drippings, scraping particles that cling to bottom of skillet. Pour warm vinegar dressing over lettuce; add chicken, and toss. Sprinkle with croutons and cheese.

❝*This salad's almost a meal in itself. Pair it with Creamy Tomato Soup (page 140)—and dinner is served!*❞

Uptown Turkey Salad

4 servings

prep: 20 minutes

2½ cups chopped cooked turkey
1   cup diced celery
½   cup raisins
2   scallions, thinly sliced

½   cup mayonnaise or salad dressing
¼   cup chopped fresh parsley
1   tablespoon dry white wine or
        1 tablespoon chicken broth
½   teaspoon dried tarragon
¼   teaspoon salt
¼   teaspoon pepper

½   cup slivered almonds, toasted (see
        tip on page 41)

1 Combine first 4 ingredients in a large bowl.

2 Combine mayonnaise and next 5 ingredients in a medium bowl, stirring well. Add to turkey mixture, and toss gently.

3 Stir in toasted almonds just before serving.

66*Toasted almonds, tarragon, and a splash of white wine make this salad 'uptown.' Preparing this dish is a good way to use up any leftover cooked turkey or chicken you may have.*99

Warm Potato-and-Sausage Salad

6 servings

prep: 10 minutes   cook: 20 minutes

3   pounds red potatoes

1   pound kielbasa sausage, sliced
        (see tip)

4   scallions, sliced
½   cup dill pickle relish
¼   cup chopped fresh parsley

½   cup olive oil
¼   cup white wine vinegar or white
        vinegar
1   tablespoon chopped fresh tarragon
        or 1 teaspoon dried tarragon
1   tablespoon Dijon mustard
1   teaspoon freshly ground pepper
½   teaspoon salt
3   cloves garlic, minced

1 Cook potatoes in boiling water to cover in a Dutch oven 10 to 15 minutes or until tender; drain and cool to touch.

2 Meanwhile, cook sausage in a large nonstick skillet over medium-high heat 4 minutes or until browned. Drain and set aside.

3 Slice potatoes. Combine potato slices, scallions, pickle relish, and parsley in a large bowl; stir in sausage.

4 Combine oil and remaining 6 ingredients in a 2-cup microwave-safe measuring cup. Microwave at HIGH 45 seconds or just until mixture is very warm (do not boil). Pour warm dressing over potato mixture; toss to coat.

Note: The dressing was tested in an 1100-watt microwave oven.

"For some extra heat in this potato salad, use Andouille or other smoked sausage in place of kielbasa. That'll get the gang's attention!"

Double-decker Club Sandwiches

4 servings

prep: 18 minutes

½ cup sour cream
1½ tablespoons prepared horseradish
1 teaspoon honey mustard
⅛ teaspoon garlic salt
Dash of ground white pepper

¾ pound thinly sliced cooked ham
12 slices whole wheat bread, toasted
4 (1-ounce) slices Swiss cheese
8 leaf lettuce leaves
¾ pound sliced cooked turkey
8 slices tomato
4 slices bacon, cooked

16 pimiento-stuffed olives

1 Combine first 5 ingredients in a medium bowl.

2 Layer ham evenly on 4 slices of bread. Top each with 1 heaping teaspoon sour cream mixture, 1 slice cheese, 1 lettuce leaf, and another slice of bread. Layer turkey evenly over sandwiches, and top each with 1 heaping teaspoon sour cream mixture, 1 lettuce leaf, 2 slices of tomato, and 1 slice of bacon. Top with remaining slices of bread.

3 Skewer 1 olive onto each of 16 sandwich picks. Cut each sandwich into 4 triangles, and secure each triangle with a sandwich pick.

❝You'll save time—and nutrients—
by leaving the peel on the tomato.
Just slice away!❞

Chicken-Avocado Dagwoods

(pictured on page 39)

4 servings

prep: 25 minutes   cook: 6 minutes

8   slices bacon

Mayonnaise
8   slices sourdough bread, toasted
2   ripe avocados, peeled and mashed
        (see tip)
8   lettuce leaves
8   (¼"-thick) slices roasted chicken
        breast
4   (1-ounce) slices Monterey Jack or
        provolone cheese
8   slices tomato
8   slices red onion
⅛   teaspoon salt
⅛   teaspoon pepper
Garnish: sweet pickles

1 Place bacon on a microwave-safe rack in a microwave-safe baking dish; cover with paper towels. Microwave at HIGH 6 minutes or until bacon is crisp. Drain bacon, and set aside.

2 Spread mayonnaise on toast. Layer mashed avocados, lettuce, chicken, cheese, tomato and onion slices, and bacon on 4 slices toast. Sprinkle with salt and pepper. Top with remaining toast. Garnish, if desired. Serve immediately.

Note: Bacon was tested in an 1100-watt microwave oven.

Mashed Avocados
Try this clean and easy way to mash avocados: Place the peeled avocado halves in a resealable plastic freezer bag; seal bag, and squeeze away!

Pesto Focaccia Sandwich

6 servings

prep: 10 minutes   cook: 10 minutes

1   large deli-loaf focaccia or ciabatta
     bread
1   (3½-ounce) jar prepared pesto
     sauce
½   pound thinly sliced Black Forest
     ham
½   pound thinly sliced roasted turkey
     breast
6   slices provolone cheese
½   small red onion, thinly sliced

1 Preheat the oven to 450°. Cut bread in half horizontally, using a serrated knife. Spread pesto evenly over cut sides. Layer ham and remaining 3 ingredients evenly over bottom half. Top with remaining bread half. Wrap with aluminum foil.

2 Bake at 450° for 10 minutes. Cut into 6 wedges.

❝This family-sized sandwich is big enough for 6 servings! Serve it with fresh fruit or a light salad for a filling meal.❞

Monte Cristo Sandwiches

3 servings

prep: 10 minutes   cook: 24 minutes

1½ tablespoons mayonnaise
¾   teaspoon prepared mustard
6   slices sandwich bread, trimmed
3   slices cooked turkey
3   slices cooked ham
3   slices Swiss cheese

1   large egg, lightly beaten
½   cup milk
¾   cup pancake mix

3   tablespoons butter
Sifted powdered sugar (optional)
Strawberry preserves (optional)

1 Combine mayonnaise and mustard; spread on 1 side of each bread slice. Place 1 slice each of turkey, ham, and cheese on 3 bread slices. Top with remaining bread. Cut each sandwich in half diagonally, and secure with wooden toothpicks.

2 Combine egg and milk in a shallow dish. Add pancake mix, stirring until blended. Dip each sandwich into batter.

3 Melt butter in a large heavy skillet, griddle, or electric skillet; add sandwiches, and cook 4 minutes on each side or until light golden. If desired, serve with powdered sugar and strawberry preserves.

❝Don't pass on the powdered sugar and strawberry preserves. They lend a pleasant and traditional sweetness to these otherwise savory batter-fried sandwiches.❞

Sausage-Stuffed French Loaf

4 servings

prep: 15 minutes   cook: 30 minutes

1   (12-ounce) loaf unsliced French
       bread

½   pound ground pork sausage
½   pound ground chuck
1   medium onion, chopped
1   cup (4 ounces) shredded mozzarella
       cheese
1   large egg, lightly beaten
¼   cup chopped fresh parsley or
       1 tablespoon dried parsley
1   teaspoon Dijon mustard
½   teaspoon salt
½   teaspoon pepper
¼   teaspoon fennel seeds

2   tablespoons butter
1   large clove garlic, minced

1 Cut off ends of loaf; discard or set ends aside for another use. Hollow out center of loaf with a long serrated bread knife, leaving a ½" shell. Process bread, removed from inside of loaf, in a food processor to make coarse crumbs. Set bread shell and crumbs aside.

2 Preheat the oven to 400°. Cook sausage, beef, and onion in a large skillet over medium-high heat, stirring until the meat crumbles and is no longer pink; drain. Add 1 cup reserved breadcrumbs, the cheese, and next 6 ingredients; stir well. Spoon meat mixture into bread shell.

3 Melt butter in a saucepan. Add garlic; cook about 1 minute. Brush butter mixture over loaf. Wrap loaf in aluminum foil, leaving open slightly on top; place loaf on a baking sheet. Bake at 400° for 20 minutes or until loaf is heated and cheese melts. Cut into 4 pieces.

❝Impress 'em with French bread that's hollowed out and stuffed with a savory mixture of sausage, beef, and cheese. Yum-my!❞

Meatball Hoagies

6 servings

prep: 4 minutes   cook: 20 minutes

1   (20-ounce) package frozen meatballs
1   (27.7-ounce) jar spaghetti sauce
1   clove garlic, crushed

1   (15-ounce) package hoagie or
        submarine rolls, split
1½ cups (6 ounces) shredded mozzarella
        cheese

1 Combine first 3 ingredients in a large skillet or saucepan. Cover and cook 20 minutes over medium heat, stirring occasionally.

2 Spoon mixture evenly onto bottoms of rolls; top with cheese and tops of rolls. Serve immediately.

❝Having some of the gang over to watch the game? These Meatball Hoagies are hands-down winners. They're ooh-so-satisfying!❞

Grilled Pizza Sandwiches

4 servings

prep: 12 minutes   cook: 12 minutes

½   cup mayonnaise
2   teaspoons dried Italian seasoning
8   slices whole grain bread (see tip)

6   ounces packaged sliced pepperoni
1½   cups (6 ounces) shredded mozzarella
      cheese

❝Move over grilled cheese, and say hello to Grilled Pizza Sandwiches—they're a pepperoni lover's dream! *You'll want to buy a loaf of sturdy bread to contain all the ooey-gooey pizza mixture.*❞

1 Combine mayonnaise and Italian seasoning in a small bowl; spread ⅓ of mixture evenly on 1 side of bread slices.

2 Layer pepperoni and cheese on mayonnaise side of 4 bread slices; top with remaining bread slices, mayonnaise side down.

3 Spread ⅓ of remaining mayonnaise mixture on tops of sandwiches. Place sandwiches, mayonnaise side down, in a hot griddle or large nonstick skillet. Cook over medium heat until bread is golden. Spread remaining mayonnaise mixture on ungrilled sides of sandwiches; turn and cook until sandwiches are golden.

Sweet Sloppy Joes

4 servings

prep: 5 minutes   cook: 23 minutes

1½ pounds ground beef
1   small onion, chopped
1   small green bell pepper, seeded and
        chopped

1   (10¾-ounce) can tomato soup,
        undiluted
1   (8-ounce) can tomato sauce
1   cup ketchup
2   tablespoons brown sugar (see tip)
1   tablespoon Worcestershire sauce
1   teaspoon prepared mustard
⅛   teaspoon garlic powder
4   sesame seed hamburger buns,
        toasted

1 Cook first 3 ingredients in a large skillet, stirring until the beef crumbles and is no longer pink; drain.

2 Stir in soup and next 6 ingredients; simmer 10 to 15 minutes, stirring often. Serve on toasted buns.

Not-So-Sweet Joes
If *sweet* Sloppy Joes aren't your thing, simply omit the brown sugar. They'll still taste great!

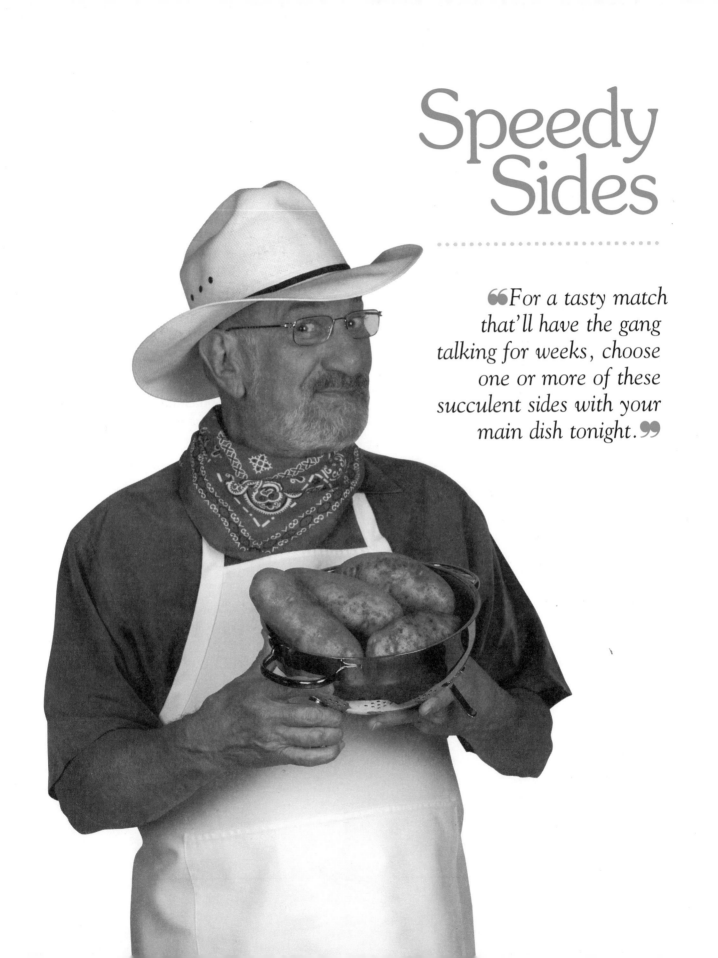

Speedy Sides

66For a tasty match that'll have the gang talking for weeks, choose one or more of these succulent sides with your main dish tonight.99

Baked Spiced Fruit

8 servings

prep: 5 minutes   cook: 32 minutes

1   (15-ounce) can apricot halves in
      light syrup, drained
1   (15-ounce) can pear halves, drained
1   (15-ounce) can peach halves,
      drained
2   (8-ounce) cans pineapple chunks or
      tidbits, drained

1   cup orange juice
⅓   cup packed brown sugar
1   tablespoon lemon juice
4   whole cloves
1   (3") stick cinnamon
Dash of salt

1 Cut apricot, pear, and peach halves
  in half; place in a 7" x 11" baking
dish along with pineapple.

2 Preheat the oven to 350°. Combine
  orange juice and remaining 5
ingredients in a saucepan; bring to a
boil, reduce heat, and simmer 2 minutes.
Pour over fruit. Bake, uncovered, at
350° for 30 minutes. Cool slightly.
Remove cloves and cinnamon stick
before serving. Serve warm.

Doubly Delicious
This casserole is an easy summer or winter dish
that's equally good hot or cold. To serve cold, bake
as directed, and then cover and chill 8 hours.

Curried Pineapple

8 servings

prep: 5 minutes   cook: 25 minutes

2   (20-ounce) cans pineapple chunks

1   cup packed light brown sugar
2   tablespoons butter
1   teaspoon curry powder
1   cup chopped pecans, toasted
     (see tip)

1 Drain pineapple, reserving juice. Place pineapple in a large heatproof serving bowl, and set aside.

2 Bring 1 cup reserved pineapple juice, the brown sugar, butter, and curry powder to a boil in a saucepan; reduce heat, and simmer, uncovered, 20 minutes. Pour mixture over pineapple, tossing to coat. Sprinkle with chopped pecans. Serve warm or at room temperature.

Toasting Tact

Toasting brings out the full flavor of nuts and also helps them stay crisp when combined with moist ingredients. Use a dry skillet to toast a small amount of nuts over medium heat for just a few minutes, stirring them occasionally. Sense of smell is key in judging when they're toasted, but watch closely—the smaller the pieces are, the quicker they cook!

Stir-Fried Asparagus

6 servings

prep: 4 minutes   cook: 12 minutes

1½ pounds fresh asparagus spears

1   tablespoon vegetable oil
¾   cup water, divided

¾   teaspoon chicken bouillon granules
1   tablespoon cornstarch
1   teaspoon sugar
2   tablespoons soy sauce
1   (2-ounce) package cashews, coarsely
      chopped and toasted (about
      ½ cup) (see tip)

1 Snap off tough ends of asparagus. Cut spears into 1" pieces.

2 Heat oil in a large skillet over medium-high heat. Add asparagus, and cook, stirring constantly, 3 minutes. Add ¼ cup water; cover and cook 4 minutes or until crisp-tender.

3 Combine remaining ½ cup water, the bouillon granules, and next 3 ingredients, stirring until smooth. Add to asparagus, stirring constantly. Bring to a boil; cook, stirring constantly, 1 minute. Sprinkle with cashews, and serve immediately.

Oven Toasting

In addition to your cooktop, your oven is a handy-dandy tool for toasting nuts. Place cashews in an ungreased pan, and bake at 350° for 3 to 5 minutes.

Garlicky Buttered Green Beans

6 servings

prep: 5 minutes   cook: 15 minutes

¾ cup water
1½ pounds fresh green beans, trimmed

¼ cup butter
1 large clove garlic, minced
Salt and pepper to taste

1 Bring water to a boil in a large saucepan; add beans. Cover, reduce heat, and simmer 10 to 12 minutes or until crisp-tender, stirring occasionally. Drain beans, and set aside.

2 Return saucepan to heat. Melt butter in saucepan, and add garlic; sauté garlic 30 seconds. Add beans, salt, and pepper; toss.

No daylong simmering is necessary for these green gems. You want to get 'em in and out of the pot fast to maximize true color, texture, and nutrients.

Cabbage Stir-Fry

4 to 6 servings

prep: 15 minutes   cook: 14 minutes

2   tablespoons vegetable oil
½   red cabbage, thinly sliced
1   green bell pepper, thinly sliced
1   small onion, thinly sliced

¾   cup chopped fresh cilantro
1   tablespoon lime juice
1   teaspoon salt
½   teaspoon black pepper

1 Heat oil in a large skillet or wok at high heat 3 to 4 minutes. Add cabbage, bell pepper, and onion; stir-fry 7 to 10 minutes or until crisp-tender or to desired degree of doneness.

2 Stir in cilantro, lime juice, salt, and black pepper.

Spicy Cabbage Stir-Fry

For an extra kick, stir in 3 tablespoons of jalapeño jelly with the cabbage, bell pepper, and onion. Proceed as directed with recipe.

Cheddar-Broccoli Casserole

6 servings

prep: 9 minutes   cook: 30 minutes

2   (10-ounce) packages frozen
      chopped broccoli, thawed and
      drained
1   (10¾-ounce) can cream of
      mushroom soup, undiluted
1   cup (4 ounces) shredded Cheddar
      cheese
1   cup mayonnaise
½   teaspoon garlic salt
2   large eggs, lightly beaten
½   cup herb-seasoned stuffing mix
Paprika

1 Preheat the oven to 350°. Combine first 6 ingredients in a lightly greased 7" x 11" baking dish. Sprinkle with seasoned stuffing mix and paprika. Bake, uncovered, at 350° for 30 minutes.

Make It Ahead

Get a jump-start on your meal by combining all the ingredients in this casserole except the stuffing mix and paprika the night before. Then cover and chill. The next day, sprinkle with stuffing mix and paprika and bake as directed.

Dilly Brussels Sprouts

4 servings

prep: 2 minutes   cook: 10 minutes

1   (16-ounce) package frozen Brussels
       sprouts

¾   cup zesty Italian salad dressing
1   tablespoon chopped fresh dill or
       1 teaspoon dried dillweed
2   scallions, sliced

1 Cook Brussels sprouts according to
   package directions; drain well.

2 Combine Brussels sprouts, dressing,
   dill, and scallions in a large bowl,
tossing gently. Serve immediately, or
cover and chill 30 minutes.

FYI

Did you ever think that Brussels sprouts look like tiny
cabbages? Well, there's a reason: They're a member
of the cabbage family—and even taste like it!

Orange-Glazed Carrots

4 servings

prep: 3 minutes   cook: 13 minutes

2   (9-ounce) packages frozen whole
       baby carrots

2   tablespoons brown sugar
2   teaspoons cornstarch
¼   teaspoon ground ginger
¼   teaspoon salt
¾   cup orange juice

1 Cook carrots according to package directions, omitting salt; drain carrots, and set aside.

2 Combine brown sugar and remaining 4 ingredients in a saucepan, stirring until smooth. Bring to a boil over medium heat; cook, stirring constantly, 1 minute. Add carrots, and cook 2 more minutes.

Bet you didn't know that cooked carrots are better for us than raw carrots. Cooking them unleashes more beta carotene, which is a form of vitamin A that appears to help reduce the risk of cancer.

Garlic-Cheese Grits

6 servings

prep: 3 minutes   cook: 12 minutes

4   cups water
1   cup quick-cooking grits, uncooked
½   teaspoon salt

1   (6-ounce) roll process cheese with
          garlic
⅛   teaspoon ground red pepper

1 Bring water to a boil in a Dutch oven; stir in grits and salt. Return to a boil; cover, reduce heat, and simmer 5 minutes, stirring occasionally.

2 Remove from heat; add cheese and pepper, stirring until cheese melts.

"Grits aren't just for breakfast anymore! Try 'em as a side dish to round out your meal. They're especially good teamed with pork and roasted chicken."

Souped-Up Mac 'n' Cheese

6 servings

prep: 5 minutes   cook: 25 minutes

8   ounces uncooked elbow macaroni

1   (10¾-ounce) can Cheddar cheese
        soup, undiluted (see tip)
1   (8-ounce) package shredded
        American and Cheddar cheese
        blend
½   cup milk
½   teaspoon prepared mustard
¼   teaspoon pepper

1   (2.8-ounce) can French fried onion
        rings

1 Preheat the oven to 400°. Cook macaroni according to package directions; drain.

2 Stir together cheese soup and next 4 ingredients in a large bowl. Stir in macaroni. Spoon macaroni mixture into a lightly greased 7" x 11" baking dish.

3 Bake at 400° for 10 minutes or until thoroughly heated. Top with French fried onion rings, and bake 3 more minutes.

❝Try nacho cheese soup in place of Cheddar cheese soup for a spicier flavor. It's 'nacho' average side dish anymore!❞

Noodles Romanoff

6 servings

prep: 5 minutes   cook: 30 minutes

1   (8-ounce) package wide egg noodles

1   (16-ounce) container sour cream
¼   cup butter, melted
¼   teaspoon salt
¼   teaspoon pepper
1   clove garlic, pressed
¼   cup grated Parmesan cheese

Chopped fresh parsley

1 Preheat the oven to 350°. Cook noodles according to package directions; drain.

2 Stir sour cream and next 4 ingredients into noodles; spoon into a greased 2-quart baking dish. Sprinkle with cheese.

3 Cover and bake at 350° for 20 minutes or until thoroughly heated. Sprinkle with parsley just before serving.

The buck stops here when looking for a versatile side dish. You can pair just about any entrée with these noodles. They're great for your picky eaters, too, when nothing else will do.

Mashed Potato Casserole

8 servings

prep: 12 minutes   cook: 30 minutes

3   cups frozen mashed potatoes
       (see tip)
1½ cups milk
1   (16-ounce) container sour cream
¼   cup frozen chopped chives
2   tablespoons minced onion
1   tablespoon prepared horseradish
1   teaspoon salt

1   teaspoon butter, melted

1 Preheat the oven to 350°. Prepare potatoes according to package directions, using 1½ cups milk. Add sour cream and next 4 ingredients, stirring well.

2 Spoon mixture into a lightly greased 2-quart baking dish, and drizzle with melted butter.

3 Bake, uncovered, at 350° for 30 minutes or until thoroughly heated.

Potato Pointers
Tap the bag of frozen potatoes on the countertop, and knead gently to break them apart. This will make the potatoes easier to measure without having to thaw.

Basil and Tomato Couscous

6 servings

prep: 20 minutes

1¼ cups boiling water
1¼ cups couscous, uncooked (see tip)

1 cup finely chopped fresh basil
⅓ cup finely chopped red onion
3 slices bacon, cooked and crumbled
2 medium tomatoes, seeded and
    chopped

¼ cup cider vinegar
2 tablespoons olive oil
¼ teaspoon salt
¼ teaspoon pepper

1 Combine boiling water and couscous in a large heatproof bowl; cover and let stand 5 minutes. Uncover and fluff with a fork; cool slightly.

2 Add basil and next 3 ingredients to couscous; stir well.

3 Combine vinegar and remaining 3 ingredients in a jar; cover tightly, and shake vigorously. Drizzle vinegar mixture over couscous mixture, and toss gently. Serve immediately; or for more flavor, cover and chill at least 2 hours. Toss gently before serving.

What's Couscous?

Pronounced "koos-koos," it's a tiny, bead-shaped pasta that's popular in Mediterranean and Middle Eastern cooking. Look for this quick-cooking pasta with the rice and grains at your supermarket.

Dressed-Up Wild Rice

4 servings

prep: 5 minutes   cook: 20 minutes

1   tablespoon butter
1   cup sliced fresh mushrooms
3   scallions, sliced

1   (6.2-ounce) package quick long-
     grain and wild rice mix (including
     seasoning packet), uncooked
1⅔ cups water
⅓   cup sherry (see tip)

1 Melt butter in a large skillet over medium-high heat. Add mushrooms and scallions, and cook, stirring constantly, until tender.

2 Stir rice mix, seasoning packet, water, and sherry into vegetable mixture; bring to a boil, stirring occasionally. Cover, reduce heat, and simmer 10 minutes or until rice is tender and liquid is absorbed. Stir gently with a fork before serving.

“For this dish, a simple package of long-grain and wild rice is dressed up with sautéed vegetables and a bit of sherry. Cook with sherry like you would wine—using only ones that you would drink.”

Vegetable-Brown Rice Stir-Fry

(pictured on facing page)

2 servings

prep: 5 minutes   cook: 20 minutes

1   (3.5-ounce) boil-in-bag brown rice

1   tablespoon peanut or vegetable oil
3   tablespoons cashew halves

1   (16-ounce) package frozen broccoli,
       peppers, onions, and mushrooms

1   tablespoon cornstarch
¾   teaspoon chicken bouillon granules
½   teaspoon garlic powder
⅛   teaspoon ground ginger
¾   cup water
1½   tablespoons soy sauce

1 Prepare rice according to package directions; keep warm.

2 Heat oil in a large skillet over medium-high heat. Add cashews, and cook, stirring constantly, until lightly browned; remove from skillet, and set aside.

3 Add frozen vegetables to skillet, and cook, stirring constantly, 6 to 8 minutes or until tender.

4 Combine cornstarch and next 3 ingredients in a small bowl; stir in water and soy sauce. Add to vegetables in skillet; cook, stirring constantly, 4 minutes or until thickened and bubbly. Stir in cashews, and serve immediately over rice.

"Brown rice usually requires a longer cook time than white rice, but thanks to the convenience of instant brown rice—and frozen veggies—you can get this nutritious dish ready fast."

Tomato-Basil-Mozzarella Salad,
page 143

Decadent Mud Pie,
page 184

Grilled Eggplant

(pictured on facing page)

4 servings

prep: 5 minutes   cook: 8 minutes

½   teaspoon dried thyme
¼   teaspoon salt
¼   teaspoon pepper
¼   teaspoon dried rosemary, crushed
1   medium eggplant, unpeeled (about
        1¼ pounds)
¼   cup Italian salad dressing

1 Preheat the grill to medium-high heat (350° to 400°). Combine first 4 ingredients in a small bowl. Cut eggplant into ½"-thick slices. Brush both sides of each slice with dressing, and sprinkle evenly with herb mixture.

2 Grill, covered, 4 minutes on each side or to desired doneness.

Eggplant Sandwiches

Turn this side dish into an entrée by topping with slices of provolone or mozzarella cheese during the last 2 minutes of grilling and serving on firm rolls.

Lucky Black-Eyed Peas

6 servings

prep: 8 minutes   cook: 10 minutes

4   slices bacon

1   medium-sized green bell pepper,
        seeded and chopped
1   medium onion, chopped
2   (15.8-ounce) cans black-eyed peas,
        drained
1   (14½-ounce) can Cajun-style stewed
        tomatoes, undrained and chopped
½   teaspoon salt
¼   teaspoon black pepper

1 Cook bacon in a large skillet until crisp; remove bacon, reserving drippings in skillet. Crumble bacon, and set aside.

2 Cook bell pepper and onion in reserved drippings over medium-high heat, stirring constantly, until tender. Add peas and remaining 3 ingredients to skillet. Cook over low heat until thoroughly heated, stirring often. Sprinkle with crumbled bacon.

"Whether you're cooking up a batch of black-eyed peas for luck on New Year's Day or just looking for a speedy side, this is the recipe for you! I use canned peas packed from fresh shelled peas instead of dried peas for the best flavor."

Garden Sauté

6 servings

prep: 10 minutes   cook: 10 minutes

1   tablespoon vegetable oil
2   cloves garlic, crushed
1   small onion, sliced and separated
        into rings
1   small red bell pepper, seeded and
        cut into strips

½   pound yellow squash, sliced
½   pound zucchini, sliced

4   plum tomatoes, chopped
¼   cup fresh basil strips
1   teaspoon lemon-pepper seasoning
¼   teaspoon salt
¼   cup grated Parmesan cheese

1 Heat oil in a large nonstick skillet over medium-high heat. Add garlic, onion, and bell pepper strips; cook, stirring constantly, 2 minutes.

2 Add yellow squash and zucchini slices; cook, stirring constantly, 5 minutes or until vegetables are crisp-tender.

3 Stir in tomatoes and next 3 ingredients; cook 2 minutes or until thoroughly heated. Remove from heat, and sprinkle with cheese. Serve immediately.

"Showcase the bounty of your garden with this yummy vegetable sauté!"

Veggie Pancakes

10 servings

prep: 5 minutes   cook: 20 minutes

1   (6-ounce) package self-rising white
        cornmeal mix
1   (11-ounce) can sweet whole kernel
        corn, drained
½   large red bell pepper, chopped
7   scallions, thinly sliced
1   large carrot, shredded
⅔   cup buttermilk
1   large egg, lightly beaten
½   cup all-purpose flour
½   teaspoon crushed red pepper

¼   cup vegetable oil, divided

1 Stir together first 9 ingredients in a large bowl.

2 Heat 2 tablespoons oil in a large nonstick skillet. Drop half of batter by ⅓ cupfuls into hot oil, and cook 3 to 4 minutes on each side or until golden. Keep warm.

3 Repeat procedure with remaining oil and batter. If desired, serve pancakes with sour cream and salsa.

"For something out of the ordinary that's packed with veggies, try these pancakes for a tasty side dish. Sour cream and salsa really send 'em over the top!"

Dazzling Desserts

"Yes, you do have time to prepare dessert on a weeknight—or any night. So go ahead and indulge your gang with these quick 'n' easy delectable treats!"

Strawberry Shortcake

(pictured on page 4)

8 servings

prep: 25 minutes   cook: 20 minutes

4   cups sliced fresh or frozen
        strawberries, thawed
½   cup sugar

2   cups biscuit baking mix
⅔   cup half-and-half
¼   cup butter, melted
2   tablespoons sugar
1   large egg, lightly beaten
1   tablespoon sugar

1   (8-ounce) container frozen whipped
        topping, thawed

1 Preheat the oven to 425°. Combine strawberries and ½ cup sugar, stirring gently. Cover and chill at least 20 minutes.

2 Meanwhile, combine biscuit mix and next 4 ingredients; beat at high speed of an electric beater 30 seconds. Spoon batter into a greased 8" round cakepan; sprinkle with 1 tablespoon sugar. Bake at 425° for 15 to 20 minutes or until golden. Cool in pan on a wire rack 10 minutes; remove from pan, and cool completely on wire rack.

3 Split shortcake in half horizontally. Place bottom half cut side up on a serving plate. Spoon half each of whipped topping and strawberry mixture over shortcake. Top with remaining shortcake. Spoon remaining whipped topping and strawberry mixture on top.

Peach of a Cake
If you're in the mood for peaches, just substitute 4 cups of sliced fresh peaches for the strawberries in this scrumptious shortcake.

Easy Strawberry Trifle

about 8 servings

prep: 17 minutes

1   (7-ounce) package jellyrolls

1   (3½-ounce) package vanilla instant
     pudding mix
1½ cups milk
3   cups frozen whipped topping,
     thawed and divided

2   cups sliced fresh strawberries
     (see tip)

1 Cut each jellyroll crosswise into 3 slices; arrange slices cut side down on bottom and around sides of a 2½-quart soufflé or trifle dish. Fill in with remaining jellyroll slices.

2 Prepare pudding mix according to package directions, using 1½ cups milk; let stand 5 minutes. Fold in 1 cup whipped topping.

3 Arrange half of sliced strawberries over jellyroll slices; top with pudding mixture. Arrange remaining sliced strawberries over pudding mixture; dollop remaining 2 cups whipped topping over pudding mixture.

Sumptuous Strawberries

To prevent strawberries from becoming mushy, wash them just before using and hull them after washing.

Decadent Mud Pie

(pictured on page 175)

8 to 10 servings

prep: 10 minutes   freeze: 2 hours

1   (11¾-ounce) jar hot fudge sauce,
      heated and divided
1   (9-ounce) ready-made graham
      cracker crust
½   gallon coffee ice cream, softened
      (see tip)

Frozen whipped topping, thawed
Chocolate coffee beans, whole and
      chopped

1 Spread ⅓ cup fudge sauce evenly over bottom of crust. Spread ice cream over fudge sauce; cover and freeze about 2 hours or until firm.

2 Cut pie into wedges. Top each serving with some of the remaining fudge sauce, whipped topping, and chocolate coffee beans. Serve immediately.

Oh-So-Smooth

Soften ice cream on the counter for 5 minutes, and then stir to smooth it out before putting in pan. This gives the ice cream a creamy consistency to spread over the fudge layer of the pie.

Fudge Pie

6 to 8 servings

prep: 10 minutes   cook: 35 minutes

3   large eggs, lightly beaten
1½ cups sugar
¾   cup chopped pecans
⅓   cup all-purpose flour
⅓   cup unsweetened cocoa
¾   cup butter, melted
½   teaspoon vanilla extract

1   unbaked 9" pastry shell
Vanilla ice cream (optional)

1 Preheat the oven to 350°. Combine first 7 ingredients in a medium bowl.

2 Pour mixture into pastry shell. Bake at 350° for 35 minutes or until set. Serve with ice cream, if desired.

❝Fudge Pie, oh my! You better dish up 2 pies if you want to enjoy a slice for yourself!❞

Praline Cream-Pecan Pie

6 servings

prep: 4 minutes   cook: 15 minutes

1   (32-ounce) frozen pecan pie

½   cup whipping cream
1   teaspoon praline liqueur or Kahlúa
       (see tip)
½   teaspoon vanilla extract
2   tablespoons powdered sugar

¼   cup plus 2 tablespoons praline
       liqueur or Kahlúa, divided (see tip)

1 Preheat the oven; bake pie according to package directions.

2 Meanwhile, combine whipping cream, 1 teaspoon liqueur, and vanilla in a small mixing bowl; beat at medium speed of an electric beater until foamy. Add powdered sugar, beating until soft peaks form. Cover and chill until ready to serve.

3 Drizzle each serving of pie with 1 tablespoon praline liqueur. Top with whipped cream mixture.

Substitute Savvy
Look for praline liqueur at your local liquor store. If you'd rather use a substitute, try caramel ice cream topping, although it will be a little thicker.

Chocolate-Peanut Butter Pizza

16 servings

prep: 5 minutes   cook: 25 minutes

1   (18-ounce) package refrigerated
       sliceable sugar cookie dough

½   cup creamy peanut butter
1¼ cups milk chocolate-and-peanut
       butter chips
¼   cup miniature candy-coated
       chocolate pieces
¼   cup chopped salted peanuts
Hot fudge sauce

1 Preheat the oven to 350°. Spread dough evenly on bottom and up sides of a lightly greased 12" pizza pan (see tip).

2 Bake at 350° on bottom rack for 20 to 25 minutes or until golden. Remove from oven, and cool 15 minutes.

3 Spread peanut butter evenly on cookie. Sprinkle with chips, chocolate pieces, and peanuts. Cut into 16 wedges, and place on individual plates. Drizzle with warmed hot fudge sauce.

Sticky Fingers
Dust your fingertips with powdered sugar when you spread the cookie dough to prevent sticking.

Creamy Dutch Apple Dessert

8 servings

prep: 10 minutes   cook: 18 minutes

1   cup graham cracker crumbs (see tip)
3   tablespoons butter, melted

1   (14-ounce) can sweetened
        condensed milk
¼   cup lemon juice
1   (8-ounce) container sour cream
1   (21-ounce) can apple pie filling

¼   cup chopped walnuts, toasted
½   teaspoon ground cinnamon

1 Preheat the oven to 400°. Combine cracker crumbs and butter in a small bowl; press mixture firmly into bottom of an 8" square baking dish.

2 Combine condensed milk and lemon juice in a medium bowl; stir in sour cream. Spread mixture evenly over crust; top with pie filling. Bake at 400° for 18 minutes.

3 Combine walnuts and cinnamon; sprinkle over baked pie filling. Serve warm.

Rollin', Rollin', Rollin'

Try a rolling pin in place of a food processor to crush the graham crackers into crumbs. Place the crackers in a large resealable plastic freezer bag, and seal. Then crush away with your rolling pin. It's that easy—with little mess!

Quick Apple Bundles

4 servings

prep: 10 minutes   cook: 20 minutes

½   (15-ounce) package refrigerated pie
     crusts
1   (12-ounce) package frozen spiced
     apples, thawed
1   egg white, lightly beaten
Sugar

1   (12-ounce) jar butterscotch topping,
     warmed

1 Preheat the oven to 425°. Unroll pie crust according to package directions. Cut into fourths. Place apples evenly in center of each fourth. Pull corners over apples, pinching to seal. Place on a baking sheet; brush evenly with egg white, and sprinkle with sugar.

2 Bake at 425° for 18 to 20 minutes or until golden. Serve warm with butterscotch topping.

❝Refrigerated pie crust and frozen apples let you get this dessert ready for the oven in 10 minutes. Bake it while you eat dinner, and a nice warm dessert will be waiting!❞

Cherry Crumble

4 to 6 servings

prep: 7 minutes   cook: 6 minutes

¾   cup quick-cooking oats, uncooked
½   cup all-purpose flour
½   cup packed brown sugar
½   teaspoon ground cinnamon
⅓   cup cold butter, cut into pieces

1   (21-ounce) can cherry pie filling
½   teaspoon almond extract
Vanilla ice cream

1 Combine first 4 ingredients in a medium bowl. Cut in butter with a pastry blender or 2 forks until mixture is crumbly.

2 Combine pie filling and almond extract in a greased 1-quart microwave-safe baking dish. Sprinkle with crumb mixture. Microwave, uncovered, at HIGH 6 minutes or until thoroughly heated. Top each serving with ice cream.

Note: This recipe was tested in an 1100-watt microwave oven.

It's Your Call
Get ahead of the game! Assemble this dessert early in the day, and then just pop it in the microwave right after dinner. Of course, you could just wait and do the whole thing after dinner. It's right—and easy—either way!

Easy Pecan Tarts

8 servings

prep: 10 minutes   cook: 18 minutes

2   large eggs, lightly beaten
1   cup chopped pecans
¾   cup packed brown sugar
2   tablespoons butter, melted
1   teaspoon vanilla extract
Pinch of salt

8   (2") unbaked tart shells

1 Preheat the oven to 425°. Combine first 6 ingredients in a medium bowl.

2 Spoon pecan mixture into tart shells. Place filled shells on a baking sheet. Bake at 425° for 16 to 18 minutes or until filling is set. Cool completely on a wire rack.

❝Wow your guests with these fancy delights that can be whipped up in minutes. For a special touch, top 'em with whipped cream and pecan halves.❞

Matzoh-and-Honey Fritters

16 fritters

prep: 15 minutes   cook: 4 minutes per batch

1   (10-ounce) package plain matzoh
2¼ cups water
5   large eggs, lightly beaten
½   cup golden raisins or chopped dried
      plums
½   cup sugar
1   teaspoon vanilla extract
½   to 1 teaspoon ground cinnamon

Vegetable oil

½   cup honey
1   cup chopped walnuts, toasted

1 Break matzoh into pieces, and place in a large bowl. Cover with 2¼ cups water; let stand 5 minutes or until matzoh is softened. Add eggs and next 4 ingredients, stirring until blended.

2 Pour oil to a depth of 2" into a large skillet, and heat to 375°. Drop batter by ¼ cupfuls into hot oil; fry in batches 2 minutes on each side or until golden and done in center. Drain on paper towels.

3 Arrange fritters on a serving platter. Drizzle evenly with honey; sprinkle with chopped toasted walnuts. Serve immediately.

Matzoh Matter

Matzoh is a brittle flat bread made from just water and flour and baked without any leavening. It's traditionally served during Passover. Look for it in the ethnic section of large supermarkets.

Candy Wrap Cookies

about 2 dozen

prep: 10 minutes   cook: 14 minutes

1   (18-ounce) package refrigerated
      sliceable sugar cookie dough
1   (8-ounce) package miniature
      chocolate-coated caramel and
      creamy nougat bars

Unsweetened cocoa (optional)

1 Preheat the oven to 350°. Cut sugar
cookie dough into ¼" slices. Wrap
each slice around 1 miniature candy bar.
Place on ungreased baking sheets.

2 Bake at 350° for 13 to 14 minutes.
Cool 1 minute; remove to a wire
rack. Dust with unsweetened cocoa,
if desired.

*"Two ingredients are all that's
required to whip up these delightful
treats!"*

Chocolate-Rum Balls

about 4 dozen

prep: 20 minutes

1   (9-ounce) package chocolate wafers, crushed
1   cup finely chopped pecans
1   cup sifted powdered sugar
¼   cup dark rum (see tip)
¼   cup light corn syrup

Additional sifted powdered sugar

1 Combine first 3 ingredients in a large bowl; stir in rum and corn syrup.

2 Shape mixture into 1" balls, and roll in additional powdered sugar. Store balls in an airtight container in the refrigerator up to 1 month.

A Sure Crowd-pleaser
Chocolate wafers serve as the base of this showy candy. I don't recommend using rum extract as a substitute, so serve these at adult-only gatherings.

Microwave Peanut Toffee

1 pound

prep: 12 minutes   cook: 8 minutes   chill: at least 2 hours

¾   cup finely chopped unsalted
    peanuts, divided

½   cup butter
1   cup sugar
¼   cup water

1   cup peanut butter-and-milk
    chocolate chips

66*No candy thermometer needed here! Thanks to the microwave, you can have homemade toffee in just 20 minutes!*99

1 Spread ½ cup chopped peanuts into a 9" circle on a lightly greased baking sheet.

2 Coat top 2" of a 2½-quart microwave-safe glass bowl with butter; place remaining butter in bowl. Add sugar and ¼ cup water to bowl. (Do not stir.) Microwave at HIGH 8 minutes or just until mixture begins to turn light brown; carefully pour over peanuts on baking sheet.

3 Sprinkle with chips; let stand 1 minute. Spread melted chips evenly over peanut mixture, and sprinkle with remaining ¼ cup chopped peanuts. Chill for 2 hours or until firm. Break into bite-sized pieces. Store in an airtight container.

Note: This recipe was tested in an 1100-watt microwave oven.

Fancy Fresh Fruit

8 servings

prep: 14 minutes

1   (8-ounce) package cream cheese, softened
1   (7-ounce) jar marshmallow creme

3   cups sliced fresh peaches (see tip)
3   cups seedless red grapes (about 1¼ pounds)
2   cups fresh blueberries
1   peeled and cored fresh pineapple, cut into 1" pieces (see tip)
⅓   cup Cognac or other brandy (see note)

1 Beat cream cheese at high speed of an electric beater until creamy. Add marshmallow creme, and beat well.

2 Combine peaches and remaining 4 ingredients in a large bowl. Serve fruit mixture with cream cheese mixture.

Note: If you'd prefer a substitute for Cognac, use ½ to 1 teaspoon of brandy extract with enough water to equal ⅓ cup.

Quick Tips

Purchase fresh pineapple that's already been peeled and cored—it'll make this recipe even quicker. Dip the fresh peaches in boiling water for 30 seconds before you peel them—the skins will slip off easily!

Peach-Banana Blossom

3 cups

prep: 7 minutes

1   ripe banana, sliced (see tip)
1   cup orange juice, chilled
½   cup frozen vanilla yogurt or ice
      cream
1   tablespoon honey
2½ cups frozen peach slices

1 Combine first 4 ingredients in container of an electric blender; cover and process just until smooth. Add peach slices, a few at a time, processing just until smooth after each addition. Serve immediately.

66*For the ultimate thick shake, freeze the banana slices, too! Yum–my!*99

Chocolate Malt

3 cups

prep: 5 minutes

3   cups vanilla ice cream (*see note*)
½   cup milk
⅓   cup chocolate flavor syrup
2   tablespoons malt-flavored chocolate
        drink mix

1 Combine first 3 ingredients in container of an electric blender; cover and process just until smooth, stopping once to scrape down sides. Stir in drink mix. Serve immediately.

Note: Use 4 cups of ice cream if you prefer really thick shakes.

Minty Chocolate Malt

For the chocolate-mint lovers, substitute equal amounts of chocolate-mint flavor syrup for the chocolate flavor syrup.

Baked Pears à la Mode

6 servings

prep: 4 minutes   cook: 30 minutes

2   (16-ounce) cans pear halves, drained
½   cup honey
¼   cup butter, melted

1   cup crumbled coconut macaroons or
      amaretti cookies
Vanilla ice cream

1 Preheat the oven to 350°. Arrange pear halves in a 7" x 11" baking dish. Combine honey and butter; pour over pears.

2 Bake, uncovered, at 350° for 20 minutes. Sprinkle crumbled cookies over pears; bake 10 more minutes. Serve warm with ice cream.

"À la mode *is a French term that we Americans use to fancy-up any dish that's topped with ice cream, such as these pears. Ooh-la-la!"*

Brown Sugar-Baked Pineapple

4 servings

prep: 10 minutes   cook: 17 minutes

½   cup lemon juice
⅓   cup honey
⅛   cup packed light brown sugar

1   fresh pineapple, peeled and cored

2   cups vanilla ice cream

1 Preheat the broiler. Stir together first 3 ingredients in a small bowl; let stand 10 minutes.

2 Meanwhile, cut pineapple into 8 (½"- to ¾"-thick) slices.

3 Place pineapple slices on an aluminum foil-lined rimmed baking sheet, and pour honey mixture evenly over top. Broil 3" from heat 15 to 17 minutes or until golden. Serve with ice cream.

❝For a wonderfully sweet ending to your meal, wow the gang with this dessert. And don't forget the ice cream!❞

Cantaloupe Sundaes

8 servings

prep: 15 minutes   cook: 3 minutes

2   teaspoons cornstarch
2   tablespoons water
1   (10-ounce) package frozen
      raspberries, thawed

2   cantaloupes, peeled and cut into
      4 wedges each (see tip)
1   quart vanilla ice cream

1 Combine cornstarch and water in a medium saucepan over medium-high heat. Add raspberries; bring to a boil. Cook, stirring constantly, 1 minute. Cool.

2 To serve, fill each cantaloupe wedge with a scoop of ice cream. Spoon raspberry mixture over ice cream.

Choosing Cantaloupe
To select the best melon, shake it and listen for the rattle of seeds. Pick a cantaloupe with a soft stem end, which has a light yellow ridged or smooth outer shell. A melon with a green cast won't do.

Brown Sugar Bananas

6 servings

prep: 10 minutes   cook: 10 minutes

¼   cup butter
4   medium bananas, peeled and sliced
½   cup packed brown sugar
½   cup cane or maple syrup
½   teaspoon ground cinnamon

½   cup whipping cream, whipped
¼   cup sweetened flaked coconut,
        toasted (see note)

1 Melt butter in a large skillet over medium-high heat. Add sliced bananas and next 3 ingredients; sauté mixture 5 minutes or until sugar melts.

2 Spoon banana mixture into serving bowls; top with whipped cream and toasted coconut.

Note: Toast coconut in a skillet over medium heat 1 to 2 minutes, stirring constantly, until golden.

❝There's lip-smackin' goodness in every bite of this decadent dessert! Serve it over your favorite pound cake or ice cream.❞

Homemade Caramel Sauce

2½ cups

prep: 2 minutes   cook: 5 minutes

¾   cup butter
1½ cups packed brown sugar

1   cup whipping cream

1 Combine butter and brown sugar in a heavy saucepan; cook over medium heat, stirring constantly, until sugar dissolves.

2 Gradually add whipping cream; cook, stirring constantly, until mixture comes to a boil. Remove from heat, and cool slightly. Serve warm over ice cream, gingerbread, or pound cake.

66*You can make homemade sauce in about the same amount of time it would take to heat up a jar of store-bought sauce—and it tastes sooo much better!*99

METRIC EQUIVALENTS

The recipes that appear in this cookbook use the standard United States method for measuring liquid and dry or solid ingredients (teaspoons, tablespoons, and cups). The information in the following charts is provided to help cooks outside the U.S. successfully use these recipes. All equivalents are approximate.

EQUIVALENTS FOR DIFFERENT TYPES OF INGREDIENTS

A standard cup measure of a dry or solid ingredient will vary in weight depending on the type of ingredient. A standard cup of liquid is the same volume for any type of liquid. Use the following chart when converting standard cup measures to grams (weight) or milliliters (volume).

Standard Cup	Fine Powder	Grain	Granular	Liquid Solids	Liquid
	(ex. flour)	(ex. rice)	(ex. sugar)	(ex. butter)	(ex. milk)
1	140 g	150 g	190 g	200 g	240 ml
¾	105 g	113 g	143 g	150 g	180 ml
⅔	93 g	100 g	125 g	133 g	160 ml
½	70 g	75 g	95 g	100 g	120 ml
⅓	47 g	50 g	63 g	67 g	80 ml
¼	35 g	38 g	48 g	50 g	60 ml
⅛	18 g	19 g	24 g	25 g	30 ml

DRY INGREDIENTS BY WEIGHT

(To convert ounces to grams, multiply the number of ounces by 30.)

1 oz	=	¹⁄₁₆ lb	=	30 g
4 oz	=	¼ lb	=	120 g
8 oz	=	½ lb	=	240 g
12 oz	=	¾ lb	=	360 g
16 oz	=	1 lb	=	480 g

LENGTH

(To convert inches to centimeters, multiply the number of inches by 2.5.)

1 in			=	2.5 cm		
6 in	=	½ ft	=	15 cm		
12 in	=	1 ft	=	30 cm		
36 in	=	3 ft	= 1 yd	=	90 cm		
40 in			=	100 cm	=	1 meter

LIQUID INGREDIENTS BY VOLUME

¼ tsp					=	1 ml	
½ tsp					=	2 ml	
1 tsp					=	5 ml	
3 tsp	=	1 tbls		= ½ fl oz	=	15 ml	
		2 tbls	= ⅛ cup	= 1 fl oz	=	30 ml	
		4 tbls	= ¼ cup	= 2 fl oz	=	60 ml	
		5⅓ tbls	= ⅓ cup	= 3 fl oz	=	80 ml	
		8 tbls	= ½ cup	= 4 fl oz	=	120 ml	
		10⅔ tbls	= ⅔ cup	= 5 fl oz	=	160 ml	
		12 tbls	= ¾ cup	= 6 fl oz	=	180 ml	
		16 tbls	= 1 cup	= 8 fl oz	=	240 ml	
		1 pt	= 2 cups	= 16 fl oz	=	480 ml	
		1 qt	= 4 cups	= 32 fl oz	=	960 ml	
				33 fl oz	=	1000 ml	= 1 liter

COOKING/OVEN TEMPERATURES

	Fahrenheit	Celsius	Gas Mark
Freeze Water	32° F	0° C	
Room Temperature	68° F	20° C	
Boil Water	212° F	100° C	
Bake	325° F	160° C	3
	350° F	180° C	4
	375° F	190° C	5
	400° F	200° C	6
	425° F	220° C	7
	450° F	230° C	8
Broil			Grill

Index

FAVORITE RECIPES

Jot down the family's and your favorite recipes here for handy-dandy, fast reference.
And don't forget to include the dishes that drew "oohs" and "aahs" when you had the gang over.

Recipe	Source/Page	Remarks